ICONIX PROCESS ROADMAPS

DOUG ROSENBERG

FINGERPRESS LTD
LONDON

ICONIX Process Roadmaps

ISBN (pbk): 978-0-9564925-0-0

Published by Fingerpress Ltd (UK)
First Edition

Production Editor: Matt Stephens
Technical Reviewer: Ben Constable
Sparx Systems Marketing Coordinator: Estelle Bell
Copy Editor: Madeleine Horobin
Production Manager: Michelle Stephens
Editorial Assistant: Artica Ham

www.fingerpress.co.uk

The 3 Roadmaps are also available as ebooks from Sparx Systems: www.sparxsystems.com

Fingerpress books may be purchased in bulk for academic, corporate, or promotional use. eBook versions and licenses are also available. Please see our Special Bulk Sales web page at:
www.fingerpress.co.uk/bulk-sales.html

Roadmaps at a Glance

Contents

ROADMAP #2: ICONIX PROCESS FOR EMBEDDED SYSTEMS 65

ROADMAP #3: ICONIX PROCESS FOR SOA 155

Foreword

So What's a Process Roadmap, and Why Are There So Many of Them in This Book?

At least a decade ago, as a member of the Rational partner program, I was invited to develop an ICONIX Plug-in for the Rational Unified Process (RUP). Years before that, I had been teaching our minimalist, use case driven approach to UML modeling, commonly known as ICONIX Process.

RUP was the antithesis of ICONIX Process, because it was a comprehensive library of virtually all software engineering techniques the folks who created it could think of, and then required process tailoring to produce an instance of RUP that suited some specific purpose. Being a minimalist at heart, I always thought it made more sense to start with a core subset that you knew would be useful and tailor up, i.e. add to that subset, if needed—and only if needed. So we created a plug-in that basically hid everything in the RUP browser that wasn't in our ICONIX core subset of UML, and followed the process I had been writing about in my books on Use Case Driven Object Modeling. We called it *QuickStart for RUP*. The most useful thing I learned out of this exercise was the approach of presenting the steps of the process you are following as a UML activity diagram—a *process roadmap*. We found the ICONIX Process activity diagrams (i.e. roadmaps) useful for students to follow in training workshops we were delivering.

From Use Cases to Business Processes and Algorithmically Complex Software

Fast forward a few years to where I found myself tailoring ICONIX Process for a client who was doing algorithmically complex software that had no user interface to speak of, and tailoring a Business Process Modeling approach for another client. I was also writing a series of eBooks for the folks at Sparx Systems with an idea towards making people aware of how to use some of the advanced features of Enterprise Architect such as SysML modeling, and SOA/web service development using BPMN diagrams as a front end to BPEL code generation, and exploring the capabilities of the Sparx structured scenario editor and behavioral code generation. I've never believed in teaching tools, notation, or modeling in the absence of a process, so it was natural for me to document whichever process I was working on in "roadmap" form.

The reason this book has so many process roadmaps is that there are lots of different kinds of software and systems being developed. Over the years, we engaged with many clients who were trying to solve a diverse enough set of problems. In most cases, we were able to stretch our tried and true "use case driven object modeling" minimalist process to fit the problem at hand. But as tools capabilities continued to improve, we found some common patterns in things that worked for different sorts of projects. Use case driven object modeling worked almost all of the time, because most software that gets built has some sort of user interface. But as we ran into clients who were building embedded (hardware/software) systems, algorithm intensive but GUI-less systems like image processing pipelines, developing with web services, or doing business modeling instead of software development we found good use for the set of process roadmaps we had developed.

Choosing the Roadmap That's Right For Your Project

So, which roadmap fits the problem you are trying to solve? The following guidance might be helpful:

- *For normal GUI-based software* follow *ICONIX Process for Software* (use case driven object modeling)
- *For embedded system development* follow *ICONIX Process for Embedded Systems* (SysML)
- *For algorithm intensive develoment* follow *ICONIX Process for Algorithms*
- *For business process modeling* follow the *ICONIX Business Modeling Roadmap*
- *For SOA and web service development* follow *ICONIX Process for Service Oriented Architectures*

This book both documents the various process roadmaps and illustrates their use by example. I hope you find them helpful.

About the Author

Doug Rosenberg founded ICONIX (www.iconixsw.com) in his living room in 1984 and, after several years of building CASE tools, began training companies in object oriented analysis and design around 1990. ICONIX specializes in training for UML and SysML, and offers both on-site and open-enrollment courses. Doug developed a Unified Booch/ Rumbaugh/Jacobson approach to modeling in 1993, several years before the advent of UML, and began writing books around 1995.

ICONIX Process Roadmaps is Doug's seventh book on software engineering, following *Design Driven Testing*, *Use Case Driven Object Modeling with UML: Theory and Practice*, *Agile Development with ICONIX Process* and *Extreme Programming Refactored: The Case Against XP* (all four co-authored with Matt Stephens), and two previous "Use Case Driven" books for Addison-Wesley, co-authored with Kendall Scott.

He's also authored numerous multimedia tutorials, including *Enterprise Architect for Power Users*, and several eBooks, including *Embedded Systems Development with SysML*.

When he's not writing or teaching, he enjoys shooting panoramic, virtual reality (VR) photography, which you can see on his travel website, VResorts.com.

ROADMAP #1

ICONIX PROCESS FOR ALGORITHM DEVELOPMENT

Designing the Large Synoptic Survey Telescope's Image Processing Pipelines

by Doug Rosenberg with Matt Stephens

PROLOGUE

Long Ago (and Some Galaxies Far Away)

Before we get started, here's a short summary of how I came to be involved with the Large Synoptic Survey Telescope (LSST), and an introduction to a couple of the key players on the LSST team (and good friends of mine), Tim Axelrod and Jeff Kantor.

NASA JPL: The Birthplace of Image Processing

I graduated from the University of Southern California in 1980 with a degree in Electrical Engineering and the ability to program computers in 12 or 13 different languages—and having taken only one Astronomy course (which I enjoyed quite a lot). I bounced around between a couple of aerospace companies in Southern California and a VLSI CAD company in Silicon Valley for a few years, and discovered that:

- 5% of the people in high–tech knew everything, and did 95% of the work
- I had absolutely no stomach for company politics
- Bad technical decisions made for political reasons on my projects kept me up at night
- Consultants/contract programmers made double the salary of regular employees
- I had the ability to create software of significant value

Given these discoveries, it seemed to make sense to become a contract programmer, double my salary, and invest the extra money in starting my own business to create software (and only hire "top 5%" overachievers). It took me a couple of years to figure out what kind of software I wanted to create, and I finally settled on developing better tools for programmers.

So 25 years ago (1984), I found myself as a contract programmer at the NASA Jet Propulsion Laboratory (JPL) working in a lab called the Multi-Mission Image Processing Laboratory.[1] This happened to be the lab that was processing the photos received by Voyager as it passed Jupiter, Saturn, Uranus, and Neptune. I wasn't personally doing image processing, I was working on a command-and-control system that did something called Tactical Data Fusion, where we would take all sorts of different information, fuse it together, and display it on a map. But I was surrounded by folks who were doing real image processing and I always found it to be interesting stuff. Plus the giant photo of Jupiter's Red Spot[2] on the wall of the office where I worked was pretty cool. It's possible that somebody, somewhere was doing image processing before JPL, but they started doing it in 1966, so MIPL was certainly one of the places where the image processing techniques now being used on LSST were developed.

I worked four 10-hour days a week at JPL, and spent the rest of my time starting ICONIX. I had bought a Lisa 2/10 computer (the predecessor to the Macintosh, which came out in 1984) that had a 32 bit processor, 2 Megabytes of RAM, and a 10 Megabyte hard disk, which was a lot of computer for $10,000 back then. Our department VAX 11/780 minicomputer supported 16 concurrent users on something like a single megabyte of RAM. By contrast, the topic of this book is an image processing system that will process 20 Terabytes of data every night for a decade.

NASA Johnson—Space Station SSE

ICONIX changed from being a pipe dream to a real business in 1986-87 after I met Jeff Kantor at a conference in Seattle called the Structured Development Forum (OO methodologies hadn't been invented yet). Jeff was working near NASA Johnson in Houston, defining the common Software Support Environment (SSE) for the Space Station.[3]

Jeff wanted an option for developers to use Macintosh computers, and ICONIX was just about the only game in town. We opened an office after Jeff bought 88 licenses of our Mac CASE tools (called ICONIX PowerTools), and ICONIX became a real company. Jeff is now the LSST Data Management Project Manager, and a key player in this story.

---

[1] www-mipl.jpl.nasa.gov

[2] http://photojournal.jpl.nasa.gov/catalog/PIA02259

[3] www.nasa.gov/mission_pages/station/main/index.html

NASA Goddard—Hubble Repair Project

A quick check of the NASA website shows that the first servicing mission to the Hubble Space Telescope was flown in December 1993 (another servicing mission is about to be flown as I write this[4]), which means that it was sometime in 1992 when I found myself in Greenbelt, Maryland at the NASA Goddard Space Flight Center, teaching a class on Structured Analysis and Design to the team that was re-hosting the coprocessor software.

Many people are aware that when the Hubble was first built, there was a problem with the curvature of the main mirror (it was off by something like the 1/50th the width of a human hair) that required "corrective lenses" to be installed. A lesser known fact is that the onboard coprocessors of the Hubble, originally some sort of proprietary chip, were failing at an alarming rate due to radiation damage, and part of the repair mission was to replace them with radiation-hard chips (I believe they were Intel 386 processors). The coprocessor software[5] did things like point the solar panels at the sun. So all of the software needed to be re-hosted. The Hubble Repair project was my first experience with large telescopes, and I got a cool poster to put up in my office, next to the Space Station poster.

ICONIX: Putting the "U" in UML

ICONIX spent about 10 years in the CASE tool business, and along the way developed one of the first Object-Oriented Analysis and Design (OOAD) tools, which we called ObjectModeler. Jeff Kantor had left the Space Station program and worked with me at ICONIX for a while. One of the things he did was analyze the emerging plethora of OO methodology books, looking for commonality and figuring out which of these methodologies we wanted to support in ObjectModeler. We came up with Booch, Rumbaugh, Jacobson and Coad/Yourdon, which of course includes the 3 methodologies that went into UML. We did this several years before Booch, Rumbaugh, and Jacobson got together to create UML, which happened a couple of years after I published a CD-ROM called A Unified Object Modeling Approach. So I like to think that Jeff and I put the "U" in UML.

After UML came out, it became clear to me that ICONIX as a tool vendor wasn't likely to remain competitive for very long. But I had developed an interesting training course that taught

---

[4] www.nasa.gov/mission_pages/shuttle/shuttlemissions/hst_sm4/index.html

[5] http://hubble.nasa.gov/a_pdf/news/facts/CoProcessor.pdf

people how to use Booch, Rumbaugh, and Jacobson methods together, and with the advent of UML, that class became marketable. So ICONIX became a training company, focusing on our "JumpStart" approach to starting client projects using our lightweight "unified" UML process. I also started writing books, initially *Use Case Driven Object Modeling—A Practical Approach*, with Kendall Scott, which became pretty popular.

Steward Observatory—The Large Binocular Telescope

Fast-forwarding 8 or 10 years and another book written, I received a phone call one day from Tim Axelrod at the University of Arizona Steward Observatory. Tim, in his quiet, soft-spoken way, said that he had read my book and was hoping that I might be able to pop out to Tucson and run one of my JumpStart workshops because "somebody has built a very big telescope (the Large Binocular Telescope[6]) and spent 10 years working on the hardware and completely forgot about the software, and I've just been put in charge of getting the software built." Tim is now the Project Scientist for LSST Data Management.

As it happened, the LBT class was the first occasion I had to use Enterprise Architect. I figured out how to use it on the (very short) flight from Los Angeles to Tucson. We'll tell the whole story in Chapter 1, but to make a long story short, the Sparx Systems software worked like a champ and solved the shared model issues that the (then) "industry standard" tools ignored.

As a result of the positive experience we had with LBT, ICONIX joined the Sparx Systems partner program immediately after I returned from Tucson. Our initial project was to produce a multimedia tutorial titled Mastering UML with Enterprise Architect and ICONIX Process, followed by Enterprise Architect for Power Users and we rapidly switched our focus towards training Enterprise Architect users. During this time I was also writing *Extreme Programming Refactored*,[7] the first of several books that I've written with Matt Stephens.[8]

It was during the 5-day class for LBT, where we modeled the Observatory Control System (OCS), that my whole perspective about telescopes changed. At the time, my son's 8th grade science class was grinding an 8-inch mirror by hand, and building a telescope—so that was my frame of reference when I headed for Tucson the first time. LBT has twin primary mirrors (hence "Binocular") and they are each 8.4 meters in diameter. By comparison the Hubble has a 2.4

---

[6] http://lbto.org

[7] www.softwarereality.com/ExtremeProgrammingRefactored.jsp

[8] www.softwarereality.com/MattStephens.jsp

meter primary mirror, and the big Hale telescope at the Palomar Observatory,[9] which was the world's largest for 45 years, has a 5.1 meter (200 inch) mirror.

Depending on who you talk to, LBT is either the largest optical telescope on the planet, or one of the top 2 or 3... in any event, it's BIG.[10] The Keck Observatory[11] on MaunaKea has a 10 meter mirror, but it's made in sections. On the other hand LBT being a binocular telescope means its twin primary mirrors are working together, so I'll leave that debate to the astrophysicists.

During the week, Tim arranged for me to have a lunchtime tour of the Mirror Lab at Steward. Seeing "8.4 meters" on a page doesn't really convey the scale of these mirrors. Each mirror weighs 20 tons. The Mirror Lab[12] (which is under the football stadium at the University of Arizona) has an oven that melts 20 tons of glass in an 8.4 meter mold, and spins it until the molten glass forms a parabolic shape, then they cool it down. This saves a lot of grinding time and it's a pretty unique facility. One of the LBT primary mirrors was being polished when I was there and I got to crawl around underneath it and look at it up close. When I returned to the class, those use cases that said Raise the Mirror, Lower the Mirror, Track an Object etc suddenly seemed a lot more significant. It dawned on me that getting a chance to contribute (even in a small way) to the LBT software was an opportunity that not many people get, and to have had a fingertip in both the Hubble and LBT software was really quite amazing.

Thanks to Tim, I was fortunate enough to make two trips to Mount Graham, the first when the first mirror had been installed and the second time after both mirrors were up on the mountain and they were preparing to commission the telescope. The second time, they had the Observatory Control System up and running, and LBT is now observing galaxies over 100 light years away.[13]

---

[9] www.astro.caltech.edu/palomar/hale.html

[10] See http://medusa.as.arizona.edu/lbto/observatory_images.htm to get a sense of LBT.

[11] http://keckobservatory.org/index.php/about/telescopes/

[12] http://mirrorlab.as.arizona.edu/index.php

[13] http://medusa.as.arizona.edu/lbto/astronomical_images.htm

Figure 0-1. Tim Axelrod points out a feature of one of LBT's twin primary mirrors to Jeff Kantor on one of my trips to Mount Graham. The scale is a bit deceptive, we were several floors up. You can better appreciate the size of these mirrors by noticing that there are two people down by the white railing next to the mirror.

The First Thing I Need to do is Hire a Really Good Project Manager

A few years after the class we did for the LBT OCS, Tim and I spoke again and he told me he had left LBT and was now Project Scientist for another telescope, called LSST (Large Synoptic Survey Telescope). LSST has a single primary mirror, also 8.4 meters in diameter,[14] and a 3.2 gigapixel CCD camera.[15] However, unlike LBT, LSST is a survey telescope and will continuously sweep the

---

[14] www.lsst.org/lsst/gallery/mirror-casting/Group_photo

[15] www.lsst.org/lsst/gallery/camera

entire sky rather than focusing on one spot at a time. Continuously sweeping the sky for a decade with a camera that captures 3 billion pixels in each image is what will drive the unprecedented volumes of image data that LSST will produce. So you might say that image processing was born at JPL and they're perfecting it on LSST.

When I spoke with Tim, he said: "The first thing I need to do is hire a really good project manager." I knew that Jeff Kantor was working at a company in Georgia where they were grinding him half to death with overtime, and that he needed to get out of that situation. So I told Tim that he should meet my friend Jeff. They met, and that brings us to our starting point for this story.

Lucas, Meet Spielberg

Before we start, I'd like to share one more story. Some years ago, Jeff and I were at a baseball game in Chicago, at Wrigley Field, and some drunk Cubs fans pointed out to us that Jeff bears a strong resemblance to Steven Spielberg (they did this by shouting "Hey, Spielberg!" at him for most of the game). A few years later, my son Rob observed to me that Tim has a resemblance to George Lucas. So it's almost as if I introduced Lucas to Spielberg, and we all know the results of that collaboration.

In all seriousness, I can't imagine two more qualified people to spearhead an effort to figure out how to analyze 20 Terabytes of image data per night, and it continues to be my privilege to work with both of them.

CHAPTER 1

The Large Binocular Telescope

"I've been reading your book," said the voice on the phone, "and I was hoping you might be able to come out to Tucson and give us one of your training workshops. I've just been put in charge of the software for a large telescope project, they've been working on the hardware for about 10 years and completely forgot about the software, and now I have to get it done in a hurry."

JumpStarting the LBT Software

That, as close as I can remember it, was my introduction to Tim Axelrod. Tim is a soft-spoken PhD astrophysicist from Caltech, and he's responsible for my involvement in both LBT and LSST. He's one of the smartest guys that I know, and I think we share a common distaste for dogmatic approaches to software development (and for dogma in general).

This was some time during 2002, and I was in the middle of writing my third book (which was my first one with Matt Stephens), Extreme Programming Refactored: The Case Against XP. Matt also shares my distaste for dogma; XPR is very much a "my karma ran over your dogma" sort of book.

At the time, Extreme Programming (as dogmatic as it gets) had become quite the trendy thing to do in the industry, and the CASE tool market was dominated by expensive tools that had some significant issues. The thing that disturbed me the most about modeling tools back then was the lack of a concurrent, multi-user, server-based repository. I always felt that this, combined with a high price point, was a significant impediment to the adoption of UML modeling in the field, and in a way, added a big supporting argument to XP proponents, many of whom used XP to justify not designing their software up front or documenting anything (and then skipped the hard parts of XP).

I had heard of Enterprise Architect (EA) previously, because one of their early adopters was a fan of my first book, and suggested to Geoff Sparks that he support robustness diagrams in his software, and Geoff, who is one of the most prolific builders of high quality software that I've ever met, went ahead and did so. In effect, Sparx Systems changed the whole price/performance equation in the industry with Enterprise Architect, flipping the situation from high-price/low-performance to high-performance/low-price.

High Performance and Low Price Makes a Good Combination

But back in 2002, I had never used Enterprise Architect when I got Tim's call, and as part of the preparation for the JumpStart workshop, he arranged for me to get a software license and I recall figuring out how to use it on the short flight from Los Angeles to Tucson. It seemed pretty intuitive, and my plans to spend the evening getting acquainted with the software proved largely unnecessary.

Modeling Tip: Good tools make a big difference

Don't settle for anything less than a modeling tool that's affordable, easy to use, and supports concurrent, multi-user modeling. Good tools like EA make a *big* impact on your project.

I was interested in trying Enterprise Architect because it seemed to address my two biggest issues with modeling tools at the time; price point (at that time, an Enterprise Architect license was $99 and it's still amazingly affordable) and an out-of-the-box multi-user server based repository. But when Tim told me of his plans to run it on Linux machines using a Windows emulator, and to keep the repository for the lab on a networked machine in another building (we were in the Steward Observatory on the University of Arizona campus), I was less than enthused, because I thought we were running a significant risk of JumpStarting the project into a brick wall.

A Push in the Right Direction

JumpStart is the name of our week–long training class in ICONIX Process where we work a client's real project as the lab example. Clients like Tim hire us when they need to get a software project moving in a hurry. This is a trickier process than it might first appear, because if we get the project moving in the wrong direction, it creates big problems for the client, and for us. At ICONIX, we're invested in our client's success.

Our JumpStart classes are about 20% lecture (we try to keep it simple) and 80% lab, and the lab is not a textbook example, but the real project—and most of the time a critically important project to the client. So anything that puts the lab session at risk of not going well is something that I try to avoid like the plague. I explained my concerns about the network configuration to Tim, he understood, and proposed that we try it, and if it proved problematic we'd quickly switch to plan B.

Modeling Tip: Not everything is in the UML spec

There are several really useful extensions to UML that make a big difference to a successful project. For example, **Requirements**, and **Screens** are not part of the UML, but are essential to a successful project. Easy-to-use **document generation** is also important. **Reliability** of a modeling tool is also very important.

As the week progressed, I became increasingly impressed with the capability and reliability of the Sparx Systems Enterprise Architect software. It was easy to use, never crashed once during the entire week, and had lots of useful features like built–in document generation and extended UML with important things like `Requirement` and `Screen` elements.

Having spent a decade building CASE tools, I knew a quality modeling tool when I used one, and ICONIX joined the Sparx partner program immediately after my return from Tucson. Thus began a long and fruitful association with the folks at Sparx, who continue to implement my ideas about improving process within Enterprise Architect.

ICONIX and Sparx continue to collaborate on extensions to UML and Enterprise Architect

ICONIX has developed a "process roadmap" that details all the steps of ICONIX Process on a set of activity diagrams, and a method for driving test cases (and JUnit/NUnit test code) from UML models, called "Design Driven Testing" (DDT)[16]. Sparx Systems provides excellent support for these ICONIX extensions in Enterprise Architect. DDT is supported in the "Agile/ICONIX add-in" from Sparx. Synergy between process and tools is a wonderful thing.

There's Big, and Then There's BIG

The highlight of my week in Tucson was a Thursday afternoon tour that Tim arranged at the Steward Observatory Mirror Lab. When we arrived, they were in the process of polishing the first of LBT's two 20–ton mirrors (see Figure 1-1).

Figure 1-1. LBT's twin primary mirrors each weigh 20 tons.

The Mirror Lab at Steward is actually under the bleachers of the football stadium on the University of Arizona campus. This has always reminded me of Enrico Fermi's nuclear reactor under the football stadium at the University of Chicago. If you ever find yourself in Tucson, I

---

[16] See: www.designdriventesting.com and the book *Design Driven Testing* (Apress, 2010) by Matt Stephens and Doug Rosenberg.

highly recommend taking a tour of the Mirror Lab.[17] They have a rotating oven that spins 20 tons of molten glass into a parabolic shape in an 8.4 meter mold. You've probably never seen one before.

Size Matters

While taking this tour, my jaw dropped open when I realized the true scale of LBT. It takes a big telescope to image galaxies more than 100 light–years away (especially through the atmosphere, which requires the use of adaptive optics to correct for distortion), and with that size comes complexity.

For example, because glass is not perfectly rigid, when you tilt a 20–ton mirror vertically, gravity affects the curvature of the mirror. For this reason the mirror's "skin" has devices called actuators attached to the back of it, which can either push out or pull in under software control to maintain the proper curvature of the telescope mirrors. Back in the JumpStart lab that I was running, some of my students were writing the use cases to control these actuators. Others were doing mirror pointing, aiming, and tracking. Another team (which as I recall included Tim's wife Robyn, who is now the QA Manager on LSST) was doing Telemetry use cases.

I remember thinking, as I walked back to the classroom from the football stadium, that I was pretty lucky to be involved with this project, and that between LBT and the week I had once spent working with the Hubble software folks, I was doubly lucky. I resolved to stay in touch with Tim and hoped that I might get to visit LBT one day. So far I've made it up the mountain twice, and I hope someday around 2015 I might get to visit Chile to have a look at LSST.

Stretching ICONIX Process: LBT's Observatory Control System

The Observatory Control System (OCS) for LBT was by no means a "classical" use case system, but rather a system with many realtime embedded aspects, that was controlled by an operator through a relatively simple GUI.

---

[17] http://mirrorlab.as.arizona.edu/MISC.php?navi=tours

There's a GUI, but That's Not the Hard Part

During the LBT JumpStart workshop in Tucson, the strategy that Tim and I adopted was to use the operator use cases as an organizing framework for the model, even though we knew that the user interface was not where the real complexity of the LBT software lived.

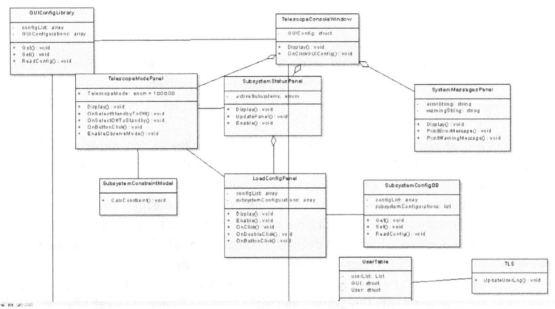

Figure 1-2. LBT's Observatory Control System GUI is not where the complexity of the OCS software resides.

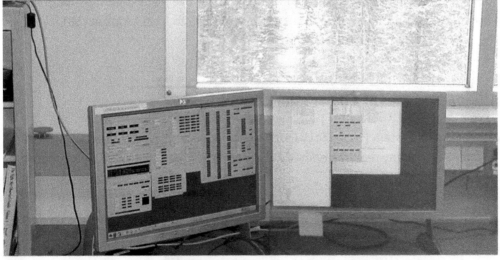

Figure 1-3. LBT's Observatory Control System does have some legitimate use cases.

Starting from the GUI, we were able to use this approach to identify "embedded operational scenarios" that were invoked from the operator–centric use cases, and recognized that within these embedded scenarios (which involve software controlling hardware), there would be some deviation from "classical" use–case–driven ICONIX Process.

Modeling Embedded Realtime Systems With Scenarios

LBT, although a behemoth among telescopes, behaves in a similar manner to most traditional telescopes in that the telescope is aimed at a celestial object, and has to track that object while the earth rotates and photos are taken. So there are various commands issued by the telescope software that drive the servo motors and other hardware that move the mirrors, the telescope (and actually the entire building that encloses it, which swivels on giant rollers) around.

While moving the telescope isn't a use case intensive process, it's fairly straightforward to identify scenarios of operation such as: "Point the telescope at a preset location on the sky" and we can model these scenarios with use cases, with an understanding that the rules for modeling use cases can be bent a little to accommodate the realtime nature of the software.

Modeling Tip: Scenario techniques work well for realtime embedded systems

Use case driven development is a scenario-based approach. It stretches reasonably well to realtime embedded systems when you can easily identify "control scenarios". Some of the "use case rules" can be bent when there is no user interface.

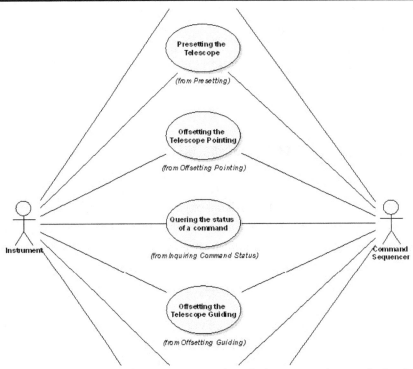

Figure 1-4. The OCS has plenty of scenarios, even though those scenarios aren't classical use cases.

So the OCS isn't really too big of a stretch for ICONIX Process because it's straightforward to identify scenarios. In general, our experience over the years has been that ICONIX Process handles realtime embedded systems pretty well. By contrast, as you'll see later, the LSST Data Management software is almost purely algorithmic in nature, making for a much bigger stretch.

Even though the scenarios are fairly simple, like moving the telescope to a pre–set position on the sky, the software within them needs to be designed pretty carefully, because software failures can get pretty costly with hardware on the scale of LBT.

Figure 1-5. Aiming the telescope involves some significant effort (Jeff Kantor explains it to my son Rob)

Modeling Realtime Systems: It's OK to Bend the Rules a Little

I had very little interaction with Tim's group after the initial JumpStart workshop until we started working together on LSST. This isn't particularly unusual with our engagements at ICONIX, as our five-day workshops are generally pretty successful at getting the UML model organized, and giving the modeling effort a big push in the right direction. But I wasn't around to guide the modeling effort, and credit for the project's success goes entirely to Tim.

Much of the benefit realized from a modeling effort is simply having a shared medium with which people on the project can communicate ideas about the design. So it's much better to do a model, and bend the rules a little, than not to do a model at all.

A good UML modeling tool like Enterprise Architect provides a shared workspace that allows different team members simultaneous access to the model, and, while providing assistance in checking semantics, is not overly intrusive about adherence to those semantics.

Modeling Tip: A shared workspace facilitates communication

UML modeling is a collaborative activity, whose purpose is to create a shared understanding of the problem and the solution. A good modeling tool that provides a shared workspace makes this communication more effective.

Tim, like many other experienced "algorithm developers" is quite familiar with using data flow diagrams to decompose complex processes, and, without me being around to harass him about staying "pure" object-oriented in his thinking, he occasionally expressed some modeling ideas in DFD-like form.

Of course, I'm no stranger to DFDs and functional decomposition myself. Back in the early days of ICONIX we built and sold a DFD editor CASE tool, and I taught many classes in Structured Analysis and Design.[18] So I recognize them when I see them, and I understand the difference between a functional decomposition with DFDs and a scenario decomposition with use cases.

I'm a firm believer that a scenario decomposition is better, in most cases, especially if the implementation is going to be object oriented, because we know how to reliably drive good OO designs from scenarios.

---

[18] This included the class I taught at NASA Goddard to the folks who were re-hosting the Hubble co-processor software.

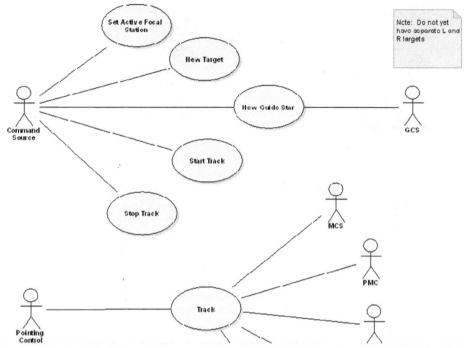

Figure 1-6. A few of the LBT use case diagrams have a distinct functional decomposition flavor to them

Semantic Consistency is a Good Thing, but It's Not the Only Thing

Successful developers and project managers like Tim (who does both) recognize that models exist to get the job done, and getting the job done comes before semantic purity in modeling.

Since it was obvious during the JumpStart workshop that the most complex part of the LBT software didn't involve very much user interaction, I encouraged Tim to bend the "ICONIX use case modeling rules" as he needed to, and use the UML model as a communication vehicle for him to communicate the design he wanted to his development team.

While the robustness diagram below (which consists almost entirely of "controller" objects— those are the circles with the arrow) probably wouldn't win a prize for semantic consistency with the textbook–specified notation,[19] it does succeed in showing the conceptual design of a group of "controller objects" interacting together to point the telescope at a desired spot on the sky (Celestial Position).

---

[19] The controllers represent verbs, or actions, in the emerging software design.

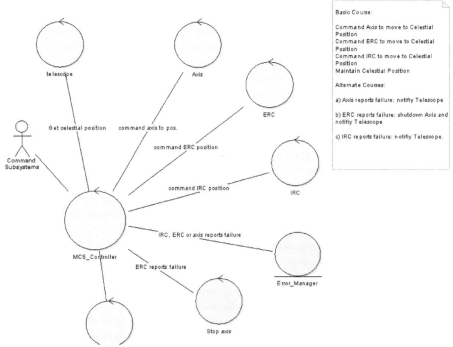

Figure 1-7. LBT's Observatory Control System is just that—a control system that uses software to control hardware. Normal "use case modeling rules" don't always apply.

It's a simple scenario, but you really wouldn't want to screw it up... refactoring the LBT hardware could get expensive. So "Test–Driven–Developing" the stopMirrors method by first making a unit test fail and running the mirrors into the wall might not be the ideal approach here.

Figure 1-8. Tim's controller objects are hauling 40 tons of mirrors (and a lot of steel) around.

Unambiguous Communication is the Only Option

ICONIX Process makes heavy use of sequence diagrams to describe a software design at an object/message level. While the process systematically drives sequence diagrams from use cases, UML sequence diagrams are still highly useful even when there are no use cases, as the "Status Request" diagram in Figure 1-9 shows.

By specifying the design at this level, Tim was able to unambiguously communicate to his developers exactly what the LBT software needed to do. To the best of my knowledge, this design is still the basis of the software that's running the LBT Observatory today.

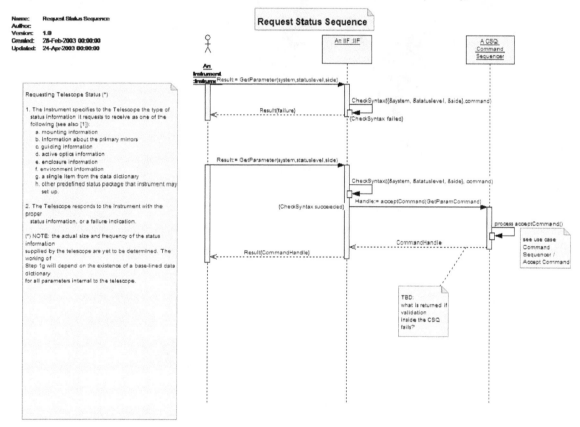

Figure 1-9. Unambiguous communication between management and developers is essential for project success.

CHAPTER 2

What's a Large Synoptic Survey Telescope... (and why do we need one)?

Many thanks to the folks at LSST Corporation[20] for allowing us to use some content (virtually all of this chapter) from the LSST.org website!

In its first month of operation, the LSST will see more of the Universe than all previous telescopes combined. Its rapid–fire, 3 billion pixel digital camera will open a movie–like window on objects that change or move; its superb images will enable mapping the cosmos in 3D as never before. Surveying the entire sky every few days, LSST will provide data in real time to both astronomers and the public. For the first time, everyone can directly participate in our journey of cosmic discovery.

---

[20] LSST is a public-private partnership. Design and development activity is supported in part by the National Science Foundation. Additional funding comes from private foundation gifts, grants to universities, and in-kind support of Department of Energy laboratories and other LSST Member Institutions. The project is overseen by the LSST Corporation, a non-profit 501(c)3 corporation formed in 2003, with headquarters in Tucson, AZ.

Figure 2-1. Suzanne Jacoby with the LSST focal plane array scale model. The array's diameter is 64 cm. This mosaic will provide over 3 Gigapixels per image. The image of the moon (30 arcminutes) is placed there for scale of the Field of View. (Image credit: LSST Corporation)

LSST's main science areas include Dark Matter/Dark Energy, Near Earth Objects, The Outer Solar System, Mapping the Milky Way, and the Transient High Energy Universe. LSST will produce and distribute a set of data products, including Images, Catalogs, and Alerts, that astronomers will use to explore these science areas.

Synoptic = All Seeing

The 8.4-meter LSST will survey the entire visible sky deeply in multiple colors every week with its three-billion pixel digital camera, probing the mysteries of Dark Matter and Dark Energy, and opening a movie-like window on objects that change or move rapidly: exploding supernovae, potentially hazardous near-Earth asteroids, and distant Kuiper Belt Objects.

Figure 2-2. LSST Group Picture. Members of the team building the LSST, a large survey telescope being built in Northern Chile, gather to celebrate the successful casting of the telescope's 27.5ft diameter mirror blank, August 2008. (Image credit: Howard Lester / LSST Corporation)

Plans for sharing the data from LSST with the public are as ambitious as the telescope itself. Anyone with a computer will be able to fly through the Universe, zooming past objects a hundred million times fainter than can be observed with the unaided eye. The LSST project will provide analysis tools to enable both students and the public to participate in the process of scientific discovery.

We've summarized some science information from the LSST website over the next few pages.[21]

Dark Matter

About 90% of the Universe is dark—we can't see it except through its gravitational pull. Although this was suspected more than 60 years ago, we are just now in a position to explore the dark matter in large areas of the Universe through a technique called weak gravitational lensing.

---

[21] You can find out much more about the science enabled by LSST at www.lsst.org/lsst/science

Dark Energy

Dark energy is a mysterious force that is accelerating the expansion of the universe. The expansion has slowed the clustering of dark matter, one of the universe's main building blocks.

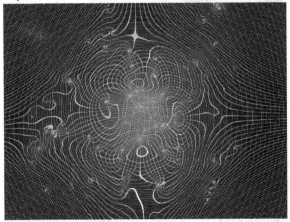

Figure 2-3. Space –time warp: the detailed mass distribution in the cluster CL0024 is shown, with gravitationally distorted graph paper overlaid. This detailed dark matter distribution can be used to constrain theories of dark matter.

Near-Earth Objects

The questions of how the solar system came into being and how life on Earth might end are two of the "nearest" astronomical issues to mankind. Answering the former requires as an initial step a census of the solar system. But identifying objects in the outer solar system has proven to be a difficult challenge despite some recent success. Answering the latter, at least in the case of a possible asteroid impact, is not strictly a scientific question but might be the most important contribution astronomy makes to life on Earth. The LSST would make uniquely powerful contributions to the study of near–Earth objects (NEOs).

The Outer Solar System

The LSST has been identified as a national scientific priority in reports by diverse national panels, including several National Academy of Sciences and federal agency advisory committees. Investigating the extent and content of the solar system beyond Neptune requires a detailed understanding of the Kuiper Belt, which in turn will lead to an improved understanding of the link between our Solar System and those being discovered around other stars. The study of the outer solar system will not only clarify the formation history of our solar system, but will point the way to how other solar systems may form and how star formation in general proceeds.

New Light On The Transient High-Energy Universe

The LSST will explore a new universe of transient sources of luminosity. We already have hints of unusual and violent events at great distances. Recently, a combination of observations with the Beppo–SAX satellite and two ground–based optical telescopes has produced proof that gamma–ray burst sources are at high redshift and so must be the most luminous objects in the universe. This must be new physics or a manifestation of physics in new and extreme conditions: attempts at a theoretical explanation using known physics have encountered major difficulties. More generally, our monitoring of and knowledge of transient sources in the cosmos is in its infancy.

Mapping the Milky Way

The LSST is ideally suited to answering two basic questions about the Milky Way Galaxy:
- What is the structure and evolution history of the Milky Way?
- What are the fundamental properties of all the stars in the neighborhood of our Sun?

LSST will produce a massive and exquisitely accurate data. Compared to the the best currently available optical survey, Sloan Digital Sky Surey (SDSS) LSST will cover an area more than twice as large, making hundreds of observations of the same region (instead of just one or two) and each observation will be about 2 magnitudes deeper. The coverage of the plane of our Galaxy will yield data for numerous star–forming regions, and even penetrating through the interstellar dust layer. LSST will detect of the order of 10 billion stars.

Figure 2-4. The 8.4-meter LSST will use a special three-mirror design, creating an exceptionally wide field of view and will have the ability to survey the entire sky in only three nights. (Image credit: LSST Corporation)

LSST Data Products

The LSST data products are organized into two groups, distinguished by the cadence with which they are generated. Level One products are generated by pipeline processing the stream of data from the camera system during normal observing. Level One products are therefore being continuously generated and updated every observing night. This process is of necessity highly automated, and must proceed with absolutely minimal human interaction. Level One data products are divided into Image, Catalog, and Alert categories, as shown in Figure 2-5.

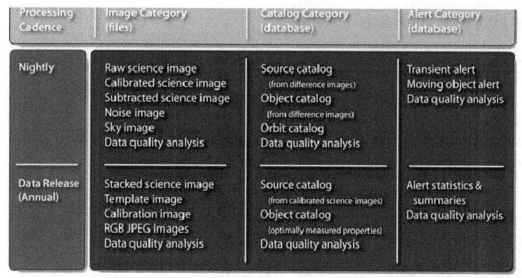

Processing Cadence	Image Category (files)	Catalog Category (database)	Alert Category (database)
Nightly	Raw science image Calibrated science image Subtracted science image Noise image Sky image Data quality analysis	Source catalog (from difference images) Object catalog (from difference images) Orbit catalog Data quality analysis	Transient alert Moving object alert Data quality analysis
Data Release (Annual)	Stacked science image Template image Calibration image RGB JPEG Images Data quality analysis	Source catalog (from calibrated science images) Object catalog (optimally measured properties) Data quality analysis	Alert statistics & summaries Data quality analysis

Figure 2-5. LSST Data Products

High Level Requirements

The Functional Requirement Specifications of the data management system include the following:

1) The incoming stream of images generated by the camera system during observing is processed to generate and archive the nightly data products

- Raw science images
- Catalog of variable sources
- Transient alerts

2) Periodically the accumulated nightly data products are processed to

- Generate co–added images of several types
- Optimally measure the properties of fainter objects
- Perform astrometric and photometric calibration of the full survey object catalog
- Classify objects based on both their static properties and time–dependent behavior

Level Two products, including calibration images, co–added images, and the resulting catalogs, are generated on a much slower cadence, and their release will be driven by data quality assessments. Although many of the steps that generate Level Two products will be automated, they need not all be so, and significant human interaction may be tolerated.

LSST Data Management Pipelines

The pipelines process the images to produce the catalogs, which are then made accessible to the community via open interfaces in a Virtual Observatory model. Since new data is being collected nightly throughout the LSST's 10-year survey period, and scientific algorithms will evolve during this time frame, significant re-processing will occur. This must be taken into account in sizing the LSST technology resources and making the LSST middleware easily extendable.

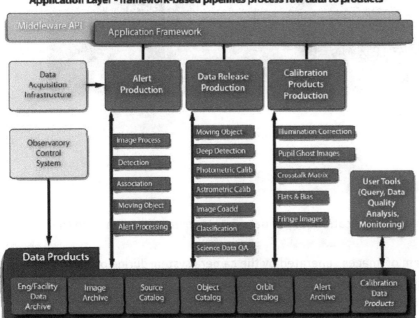

Figure 2-6. LSST's Image Processing Pipeline software is the topic of this book

The pipelines can be categorized in terms of either being near real-time or "static", depending on how stringent the associated latency and throughput deadlines are. Examples of near real-time pipelines include data quality assessment providing feedback to telescope operations, instrument calibration processing, and time-domain or transient science analysis. These pipelines execute at the mountain base facility in order to avoid the latency associated with long-haul transmission of the raw data. The static pipelines include deep image co-addition, weak lensing shear processing needed for dark energy –dark matter science, and object cataloging. These pipelines execute at the archive center. The archive center also performs re-processing of the near real-time pipelines.

CHAPTER 3

Data Challenges: From 0 to 20 Terabytes per Night

The LSST website[22] summarizes the challenge facing Jeff and Tim very nicely:

> The science archive will consist of 400,000 sixteen-megapixel images per night (for 10 years), comprising 60 PB of pixel data. This enormous LSST data archive and object database enables a diverse multidisciplinary research program: astronomy & astrophysics; machine learning (data mining); exploratory data analysis; extremely large databases; scientific visualization; computational science & distributed computing; and inquiry-based science education (using data in the classroom). Many possible scientific data mining use cases are anticipated with this database.

The LSST scientific database will include:
- Over 100 database tables
- Image metadata consisting of 700 million rows
- A source catalog with 3 trillion rows
- An object catalog with 20 billion rows each with 200+ attributes
- A moving object catalog with 10 million rows
- A variable object catalog with 100 million rows
- An alerts catalog. Alerts issued worldwide within 60 seconds.
- Calibration, configuration, processing, and provenance metadata

---

[22] www.lsst.org/lsst/science/technology

Sky Movies—Challenges of LSST Data Management

The Data Management (DM) part of the LSST software is a beast of a project. LSST will deal with unprecedented data volumes. The telescope's camera will produce a stream of individual images that are each 3.2 billion pixels, with a new image coming along every couple of minutes.

In essence, the LSST sky survey will produce a 10 year "sky movie". If you think of telescopes like LBT producing a series of snapshots of selected galaxies and other celestial objects, and survey telescopes such as Sloan producing a "sky map",[23] then LSST's data stream is more analogous to producing a 10 year, frame–by–frame video of the sky.

LSST's Use Cases Will Involve Accessing the Catalogs

LSST's mandate includes a wide distribution of science data. Virtually anyone who wants to will be able to access the LSST database. So parts of the LSST DM software will involve use cases and user interfaces for accessing the data produced by the telescope. Those data mining parts of the software will be designed using regular use–case–driven ICONIX Process, but they're not the part of the software that we're concerned with in this book.

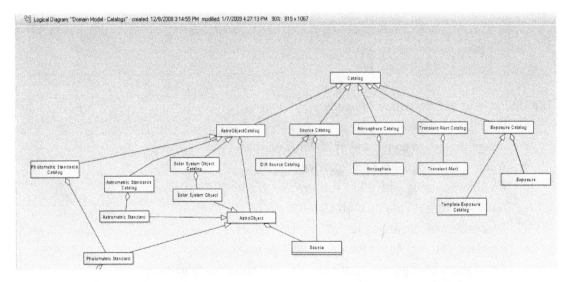

Figure 3-1. LSST will produce many catalogs, which will be widely accessible by the public.

---

[23] www.sdss.org/dr7/products/index.html

Lots of Brains and a Fair Amount of Time

There are a couple of things that Jeff and Tim do have working in their favor: plenty of brains (not only their own, but a widespread and largely brilliant team of astrophysicists that are experts on various pieces of the problem), and a fair amount of time (LSST is scheduled to go operational in 2015, and is currently in an R&D phase). However, it's safe to say that most of the astrophysicists on the team wouldn't consider themselves software engineers, although most of them are programmers. In this situation, a good strategy is to make extensive use of rapid prototyping (in this case algorithm development via prototyping) in addition to the UML modeling. So a two-pronged strategy of prototyping and modeling has been underway on LSST for a few years now.

The LSST prototyping strategy involves annual Data Challenges (see Figure 3-2). These Data Challenges are development efforts with a limited functional and performance scope, and somewhat relaxed modeling requirements. During LSST's Construction Phase, prototyping will switch to incremental development, where the actual system will be developed in a sequence of incremental releases, and somewhat more modeling will be expected.

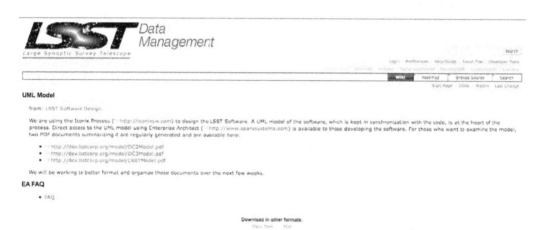

Figure 3-2. LSST's R&D Phase is being conducted as a series of Data Challenges

In the next chapter, we'll take you into a modeling workshop that I helped to conduct, for Data Challenge 3 (DC3), where the need for some process tailoring became obvious. But first let's look at some of the challenges faced by the LSST modeling team.

Let Coders Write Code

A very important part of the development strategy for LSST is to implement key algorithms and validate them, in parallel with developing an overall UML model for the LSST software. This is important for many reasons, among them (as you'll see in the next chapter) that lots of programmers prefer writing code to modeling in UML.[24] But in order to make all of these independently developed prototype pieces work together when LSST gets to Construction, we need to be able to import the prototype code into the model. Enterprise Architect's reverse engineering capabilities make this work quite smoothly (see Figures 3-3 and 3-4).

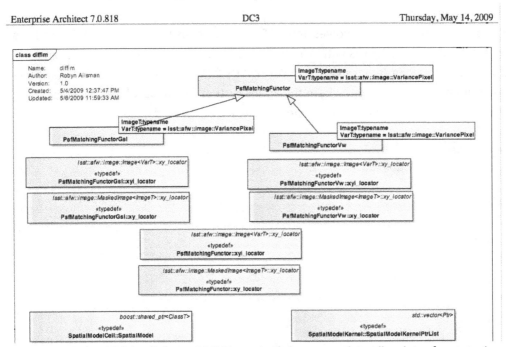

Figure 3-3. LSST's schedule allows an R&D Phase that's long enough to allow lots of prototyping.

Enterprise Architect can inhale code as fast as it can be written, so Jeff and Tim are able to allow programmers to prototype various critical pieces of the data management software during the Data Challenges, with full confidence that when the time comes to begin work on the real production software, the prototype code can be "mined" as needed and made to work within the overall system architecture.

---

[24] We know this will come as a shock to many readers.

Enterprise Architect 7.0.818   DC3   Thursday, May 14, 2009

selectBestModel	Public: void	Select best model based upon QA assesment
getCurrentId	Public: int	Get index of current model
setCurrentId	Public: void	Set index of current model
setLabel	Public: void	Set label
getLabel	Public: std::string	Get label
incrementModel	Public: bool	Go to next model in list; call its buildModel() method
isUsable	Public: bool	Is cell usable for spatial fit; false if no members or all are bad
isFixed	Public: bool	Is cell usable but the model is fixed?
_orderModels	Private: void	

Connector	Source	Target	Notes
Association	SpatialModelCell Unordered	ModelPtrList Unordered	

SpatialModelKernel

Type:	Public **Class**
Status:	*Proposed, Version 1.0, Phase 1.0*
Package:	diffim
Details:	Created on: 5/4/2009, Modified on: 5/4/2009, Author: Robyn Allsman

@brief Class used by SpatialModelCell for spatial Kernel fitting A Kernel model is built for a given Footprint within a MaskedImage. An ensemble of Kernels, distributed evenly across the image using SpatialModelCell, is used to fit for a spatial function. If this Kernel is a poor fit to the spatial function, another member of SpatialModelCell will be used instead. This class needs to know how to build itself, meaning it requires the basis functions used to create the Kernel, as well as the input images that it is to compare.
@see lsst/ip/diffim/SpatialModelCell.h for required methods

Attribute	Type	Notes
_fpPtr	Private: lsst::afw::detection::F ootprint::Ptr	< Footprint containing pixels used to build Kernel
_miToConvolvePtr	Private: MaskedImagePtr	< Subimage around which you build kernel
_miToNotConvolvePt r	Private: MaskedImagePtr	< Subimage around which you build kernel
_kFunctor	Private:	< Functor to build PSF matching kernel

Figure 3-4. Enterprise Architect's reverse engineering capabilities allow complex algorithms to be prototyped, then incorporated into the model.

Modeling Tip: Combine modeling with prototyping

Don't be afraid to build prototype code, but

Do make sure to reverse-engineer it into your production model.

Make sure your modeling tool is effective at reverse engineering.

Distributed Development Team

A further complication in modeling LSST's DM software is that the development is being done in multiple, independent, geographically distributed research organizations—places like Princeton, Stanford, University of Washington and Caltech, among others. This places some significant requirements on the modeling tools that are used by the project. Fortunately, Enterprise Architect supports distributed development using version–controlled packages, allowing someone at Caltech or Stanford to check out a package, add information to the model, and check it back in to the central repository in Tucson.

Modeling Tip: Manage distributed teams with version control

Make sure that your modeling tool allows you to manage large projects by providing interfaces to version control system and allowing check-in/check-out on a package by package basis.

Here Today, Gone Tomorrow

My involvement with LSST has been ongoing but sporadic. Due to budget constraints and the incremental nature of the various Data Challenges (and to relaxed modeling requirements during LSST's R&D phase), we never did a full 5–day LSST JumpStart workshop as we did with LBT. So my involvement has been more of an occasional visitor to the various workshops on the project, on the order of a few days a year for the last few years.

My approach has always been to show up when requested, and do the best I can to help out. In some cases this has been as simple as being "Tim's personal modeling assistant". In other cases it has involved strategy sessions with Jeff and Tim about the overall approach, and, as you'll see in the next chapter, tailoring ICONIX Process to make it work better for LSST. We'll spend the rest of the book exploring the why and how of the result: ICONIX Process for Algorithms.

CHAPTER 4

Tailoring ICONIX Process for Algorithm Development

Those of us who define software processes do our best to make a process as generally useful as possible. However, no process can be a perfect fit for every project, and while ICONIX Process has been useful to thousands of software projects over the last 15 years, there's no disgrace involved in tailoring it to fit a specific problem, or class of problems. In this case, tailoring it to fit LSST Data Management resulted in a process that's applicable to all kinds of algorithm–intensive projects.

The need to consider tailoring ICONIX Process to better fit LSST's data management software can be traced back to an email discussion between Jeff, Tim, and I back in August of 2008, in preparation for the DC3 Design workshop which was held at Caltech.

The Pasadena DC3 Workshop—How the Need for Process Tailoring Surfaced

The DC3 workshop had a very specific purpose: to bring key players from the LSST team together to brainstorm and capture ideas for Data Challenge 3 in the model. Jeff was much less concerned with the precise form that the information capture took, than with getting as many algorithms captured as possible in a short time period, because he was on the hook to produce estimates for the upcoming Preliminary Design Review (PDR).

Digging through my old emails finds this discussion, beginning with an email from me to Jeff and Tim regarding how we wanted to approach the workshop:

ICONIX PROCESS FOR ALGORITHM DEVELOPMENT

Jeff and Tim
Here are a few things that I believe help to define "the right way" to do these
use case / UML models. If left to my own devices I would teach the workshop
attendees these principles, but you need to give me marching orders as to
whether you want me to do this or not. I think one of the key values of
robustness analysis is that it helps to ensure "well formed" or "proper" use
cases. To be honest I don't know what the robustness diagrams will look like if
we don''t follow these guidelines
-use case diagrams are not Data Flow Diagrams (a use case doesn't have INPUTS:
OUTPUTS: and drill down to see lower level functions)
-to restate the previous point, use cases are a SCENARIO decomposition, not
functional decomposition
-scenarios are generally distinguished by having an actor, and represent
event/response dialog between a system and something outside of that system,
whereas functions are algorithmic (all one system)
-to restate that one, algorithms are not scenarios (algorithms are generally
represented as controllers within scenarios)
-functional requirements are not scenarios (but they should be linked to the
scenarios). Requirements can also be linked to controllers.
Doug

Tim's response to this email was as follows:

Hi Doug,
I think there's a long-term and a short-term response to your concerns. First,
the long-term. I've gradually been coming to the view that a variant of the
Iconix process needs to be developed that is better tuned to people like us
(astronomers, physicists, scientific application programmers) and the systems we
need to construct. I think that the difficulties that we've run into with LBT
and LSST are not only due to our own lack of discipline and cat-like natures.
Even those of us who support the use of a formal design process (like me) have
not really used it as intended, as you are seeing. At least sometimes, the
process just doesn't seem a natural fit to the way we think about our systems.

The part of LSST we're working on now is dominated by complex pipeline
processing, and when we scribble on our whiteboards we always end up with inputs
and outputs and boxes that transform data. And so, when we go into UML we want
to continue thinking that way, and end up torquing the design process into

something that doesn't work right. So, perhaps after PDR is complete (and we've survived it), it would be worthwhile to devote some serious thought to creating a modified Iconix process ("The Iconix Process for Scientific Cats" by Rosenberg, Kantor, and Axelrod??)

In the short term, I'm not sure how to proceed. Jeff has some pretty definite ideas of what we need to get through PDR, and somehow we need to mobilize the team to produce what''s needed. And there is the minor matter that we have a lot of code to produce as well! For the modeling, it might actually make most sense to take a subteam (say Jeff, Nicole, and me) and notionally lock us in a room to produce the model, drawing as needed on the other application folks and translating what they tell us into UML. If that's the right approach, we should try it on for size next week. Maybe there's some small modification/addition to the Iconix process that could help in the short term -you mentioned DFDs. I'll in good part leave this set of decisions up to you and Jeff, though I'll certainly want to kibitz (and maybe protest!).
Keep thinking,
Tim

So here's where it started. A suggestion from Tim that maybe it was time to think about tailoring the process. Since Tim's one of the smartest guys that I know, and I have never ever known him to speak without a good deal of forethought, I took this email very seriously, and I started mulling over what an algorithmic variant of ICONIX Process might look like.

We decided to take a day for the three of us (Tim, Jeff, and myself) to work through an example which we'd use as a model for workshop attendees. We proceeded to produce a "stretched ICONIX Process" example, which captured high–level algorithms as use cases, and lower level algorithms as controllers on robustness diagrams. I don't think any of us felt completely comfortable with the example, but Jeff felt pretty strongly that trying to introduce something other than ICONIX Process as published in my books at this particular workshop would cause more problems than it might solve, when what they really needed was some forward progress capturing algorithm detail within the model. So this wasn't the time to be thinking about process tailoring.

But all three of us knew that we were stretching "textbook ICONIX Process" further than we felt comfortable with.

As we worked through our example, the thought that kept growing in my head was... trying to model algorithms as use cases was the fundamental problem, because scenario modeling (which had worked on LBT) and algorithm modeling were different, and needed to have different guidelines. In the LSST image processing software, scenarios were scarce, and algorithms were plentiful. Tofurther complicate matters, thealgorithms were organized intoworkflows and data productions.[25]

As it turns out, the Pasadena workshop reinforced these ideas quite strongly in my mind. But it was during our day of pre-workshop preparation that I first suggested we stop using use cases to model algorithms, distinguish between workflow and science algorithms (and use activity diagrams to describe workflow, and "controllers" on robustness diagrams to capture details about science algorithms).

"We're Not Building Internet Bookstores"

I had been warned on several occasions about the level of anti-modeling sentiment in some parts of the LSST team, and in particular that one highly-brilliant "superhero programmer" was the most vocal, and that I'd be meeting him for the first time at this workshop. I won't use his name in this discussion but since he is a legitimate "superhero programmer" (being largely responsible for another major survey telescope's software), I'll refer to him as superCoder which is a fairly accurate description of his skill level. There was also another individual who, having been in the industry for quite a long time, dated back to the days of FORTRAN, and who had dubbed the robustness diagram notation "Martian" and proudly pronounced that "I don't speak Martian." For this discussion we'll call him FORTRAN_JOCK.

So Jeff and Tim had warned me to expect active resistance from superCoder and FORTRAN_JOCK during the workshop, and I was not to be disappointed. Jeff (and to some extent Tim) has spent many hours banging heads with these folks regarding the value and necessity of modeling. superCoder, having more or less single-handedly programmed the other survey telescope didn't see why he couldn't do the same with LSST. LSST, of course is massively bigger and more complex than any previous survey telescope and this would be a complete impossibility, even if it were desirable.

The first morning of the workshop turned out to be quite contentious. I had a couple of hours on the meeting agenda to present the example we had developed and give a quick overview of the plan-of-attack for the next 2 days. Jeff had predicted that this time would be used by superCoder and FORTRAN_JOCK to basically attack the whole approach we were using, and open a debate about modeling that, if left unchecked, would suck up the entire 2 days that

---

[25] In LSST terminology, "workflows" are the image processing pipelines, and "productions" involve running a set of pipelines to produce a set of data.

were allocated to capture algorithms into the model. Jeff's predictions were entirely correct, led off by superCoder's proclamation to me (and the assembled group) that he had read my book (whose example happened to be an Internet bookstore), and that while it contained lovely guidance for those who might be building Internet bookstores, that the LSST DM group was most emphatically not building internet bookstores, and thus the guidance presented in my book was generally not useful to him. This was followed by FORTRAN_JOCK's pronouncement that he didn't speak Martian, which got chuckles from everybody, including me. I now routinely introduce the robustness notation to students as "Martian".

Jeff, having fully anticipated this sort of speech from superCoder, was absolutely in no mood to tolerate it. Jeff is responsible for the LSST project passing PDR, and continued funding for the project is contingent upon the cost and schedule estimates that he needed to produce, and he needed information captured into the model during this workshop for that purpose. In a performance worthy of General Patton,[26] he stood up and basically out-shouted the naysayers and declared that we would NOT spend this meeting debating the approach, and that we WOULD spend the meeting capturing algorithm detail, end of debate, LET'S GET TO WORK.

I was privately somewhat sympathetic to the "Internet bookstore" argument because I knew we were stretching the process farther than I was comfortable with, and by then I had some ideas on how to tailor it to be a better fit to the LSST Data Management problem, but I certainly understood where Jeff was coming from, and I was quite impressed with his performance, which he had forewarned me might be coming. In any event, it worked exactly as he intended, and the workshop proceeded to capture algorithm detail for the next 2 days.

Modeling Tip—Don't confuse use cases and algorithms

Many people confuse use cases with algorithms because both are generally named with a verb-phrase and consist of a sequence of steps. In most systems, algorithms are represented as steps within use cases (controllers on robustness diagrams). LSST's image processing pipelines don't really have any use cases.

---

[26] Jeff's performance actually reminded me of one of my favorite scenes from *Patton*, one of my favorite movies. In the scene, Patton's army is marching 100 miles through the snow trying to rescue a battalion at Bastogne during the Battle of the Bulge. His officers are lamenting the bad weather and the fact that they can't get any air cover. Patton launches into a tirade that ends with: "If we are not victorious, LET NO MAN COME BACK ALIVE." His aide pulls him aside and says: "General, sometimes the men can't tell when you're acting." To which General Patton responds: "It isn't important for them to know… it's only important for me to know."

I would rate the result of this workshop as a qualified success. We captured a lot of algorithms, but we captured them in a less–than–optimal form. Essentially, the conclusion of our pre–workshop meeting was that we knew it was going to be messy, but that we'd clean the mess up later. If it had been anyone but Jeff promising that we'd clean it up later, I would have been pretty skeptical about it ever happening, but I knew he meant it. And as you'll see shortly, Tim and I were destined to become the cleanup crew, during which time the actual process tailoring took place, on a whiteboard in Tim's office.

We organized the workshop into teams, each specialized in the functional area of their particular laboratory. There were people from Princeton, University of Washington, Caltech, Stanford, and several other locations. I took charge of one lab team, Jeff took another, and Tim another, and we all floated around as best we could during the lab sessions.

The approach was to model high–level algorithms with use cases, and lower–level algorithms as controllers on the robustness diagrams for those use cases. Since the software didn't have any user interface, we didn't expect to see any boundary objects on the robustness diagrams, but we did want to use the robustness diagrams to discover missing domain objects and to identify lower–level algorithms within the higher–level algorithms. The problem with this particular project is that LSST image processing has many levels of algorithms–within–algorithms–within–algorithms–withinalgorithms and the guidance wasn't real clear when to model with a use case and when to use a robustness diagram.

To save time, we decided to have each lab team produce its own "mini domain model" before trying to describe any use cases. I was much more rigorous about this with the teams that I worked with than Jeff and Tim were, and I think it made a significant difference in the amount of progress made by the various teams. Jeff had initially penciled himself in to work withsuperCoder's lab team, but during the lunch break I approached him and suggested that I work with that team instead because the friction level between them was obviously way too high. I think that was the quickest agreement I have ever received from Jeff on anything.

As it turns out, having me work with superCoder's team was a pretty good idea. I've been developing software with Very Smart People since my college days (often PhD physicists whose science and math abilities go way over my head), and it has exposed me to some very interesting projects. I have an approach that I often use when I'm working with Tim, and it pretty much involves me starting a discussion with: "So, tell me about X" (if I remember correctly, X in this case was the Deep Detection Pipeline), and letting the Very Smart Person start explaining how it all works, while I "take notes" in UML.

There's slightly more structure behind my questions than just "tell me about the Deep Detection Pipeline" in that I'm fishing for specific information with my questions. The first thing I fish for is names of things (nouns). So while the VSP (in this case our good friend superCoder) is telling me "what are the things that are involved in deep detection", a domain model diagram is assembling itself in Enterprise Architect (see Figure 4-1).

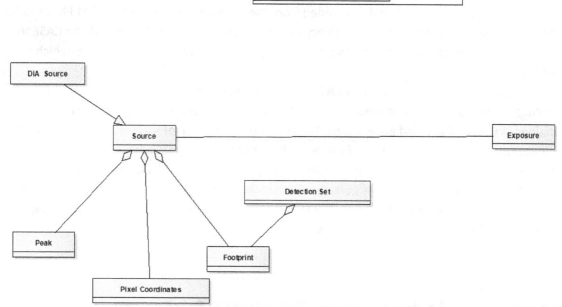

Figure 4-1. Some of the domain classes that are involved in deep detection. Note the link to a separate diagram showing reverse engineered code from the prototype Deep Detection Pipeline.

Occasionally I'll stop and ask whether the domain model I'm assembling looks right or not. The key to this approach is that I need to be able to capture information without slowing down the narrative explanation of the VSP. In this case, superCoder had already built a deep detection pipeline before, knew exactly how he wanted it to work, and was perfectly capable of explaining it at a mind–bending pace.

Modeling Tip—Always Start with a Domain Model

Failure to define your terms will always cause problems when modeling. So you should always start with a domain model. But don't get stuck trying to make it perfect upfront.

I don't like to spend too much time on domain modeling, but rather try to nail down the 80% most important domain objects as quickly as possible with an understanding that we'll continually refine this as we discover new domain classes. So after 15 or 20 minutes of domain modeling, I switched my questions over to algorithms. As it turns out, the "magic questions" for modeling use cases[27] work reasonably well for algorithms too—and I make sure any detail that I capture uses the nouns from the domain model. In this case I was trying to separate pipeline workflow from science algorithms, so I started with "tell me about the high level algorithm for the Deep Detection Pipeline" and proceeded from there. Once again, the key is that I have to be able to capture information as fast as a Very Smart Person can explain it to me, so the CASE tool that I'm using (Enterprise Architect) had better not get in my way while I'm working (which it didn't).

In a sense, I use UML and visual modeling the way a good secretary uses shorthand to capture the text of a memo or business letter. So the notation and tool that I'm using are analogous to shorthand and a steno pad. The good news out of all of this was that within 5 minutes of starting the lab portion of the workshop, our friend superCoder was standing up at the whiteboard explaining algorithms (which he was very good at and liked to do), and the algorithms he was explaining were getting captured into Jeff's model, by me. For the moment, we had overcome the resistance to modeling, but I knew that the need for process tailoring was an issue that wasn't going away anytime soon.

Tim and I Become the Cleanup Crew, and ICONIX Process Gets Tailored

After the August Pasadena DC3 workshop, I wasn't involved with LSST for several months. But as the PDR deadline started creeping closer, getting the model cleaned up started moving higher up the priority list for Jeff and Tim. So it was in mid-December that I found myself in Tucson again for a 2-day working session with Tim to try to get the model in better shape. I think all of us would have been quite happy for me to be involved with the modeling on a more frequent basis, but this was what the budget permitted. My approach was to try to be as helpful as I could within the limited time available.

I hadn't seen anything of the LSST model since August, and it didn't look like Tim had really gotten any real traction on doing much with it. Jeff had gotten the results of the Pasadena workshop inhaled into the existing LSST model, but it was sort of just sitting there off to the side, waiting for the cleanup that we all knew was necessary. My arrival was the catalyst for this cleanup to start, and Tim and I were the cleanup crew.

---

[27] As described in *Use Case Driven Object Modeling with UML: Theory and Practice*, the magic questions are: 1. What happens? 2. And then what happens? (repeat as necessary) 3. What else can happen? (repeat as necessary). These questions work well for capturing algorithms, too.

The first issue we ran into was the domain model, which was actually not a single domain model anymore but instead a collection of multiple, fragmented, and inconsistent domain models. Because of the split into multiple teams (each with a "mini domain model") in Pasadena, there was no single place to look for "the domain model" which definitively established a consistent set of names for domain classes, and the relationships between them. The domain model included reverse–engineered code from prototyping efforts, and (as on many projects that haven't discovered the power of domain modeling) names were used inconsistently throughout the model.

Tim and I ran head–first into the need to clean this up within 10 minutes of getting started. I had asked him some question which caused him to try to find something in the domain model, and it was much too difficult. It became clear to me that despite Tim having every intention of trying to make the model work, he was continually having to fight with it.

Modeling Tip: If you're fighting the model, figure out why

UML models exist to help define and communicate a development problem and its solution. If you find yourself having to fight the model, something's wrong. Take the time to figure out what the problem is, and fix it. Models should be a help, not a hindrance.

So we decided to attack this problem first, and spent a few hours printing out each and every domain model diagram, making notes on them with markers of various colors, and one by one adding dozens of objects that had been discovered in Pasadena into the projectwide domain model (renaming many of them as we went as name usage had been inconsistent previously).

We also removed reverse–engineered code from the domain model into a separate package, but grabbed the names of some of these classes and added those to the domain model. Within a few hours we saw a noticeable improvement.

Modeling Tip: Keep reverse engineered code separate from the domain model

It's OK to prototype code and reverse engineer it into a UML model. On systems like LSST, it's essential. But don't mix the reverse engineered classes with the domain model.

As the consolidated domain model grew, I suggested to Tim that it was really pretty important for him to add definitions to all the domain classes, and he agreed (with some reluctance, because it was a lot of work). He was heading to a conference in some remote place the next week and promised to spend some time adding the definitions, because he saw the value in having a project glossary. I received an email from him while he was in the middle of this exercise that said:

```
Would you believe it? The exercise of writing the definitions is turning up some
more domain objects... Tim
```

He later told me that "some more" was really about a 20% increase in the number of domain objects discovered, just by adding definitions to the classes. So, if you look for high-leverage modeling activities, like I do, this is definitely one to make a note about. Define your project vocabulary, it works. Thanks to Tim's continued efforts (with some help from Robyn), the LSST Domain Model is now an extremely useful section of the model.

Modeling Tip: Use your domain model as a project glossary

Trust me, you'll be glad you defined your domain classes unambiguously. It generally only takes a few hours, and pays dividends over the lifetime of your project.

Once the domain model got consolidated, the next thing we needed to do was to bring all of the "use cases" and robustness diagrams from the Pasadena workshop in-line with the (now standardized) domain terminology. This was no small task, certainly not one that could be completed by Tim and I in less than two days, and it was during our initial attempts at this that I became convinced that the process tailoring couldn't wait much longer.

I hadn't seen the model since August, and during the workshop in Pasadena I was mostly focused on the models produced by the teams that I worked with. As Tim and I started digging, here's what we found:

Pipeline workflows were modeled as use cases. Use case diagrams were used to describe the various pipeline stages and how they related together.

Algorithms (pipeline stages) were also modeled as use cases. So when you looked at a diagram it wasn't easy to tell if you were looking at a pipeline, a pipeline stage, or a science algorithm. Everything looked the same.

"Schizophrenic" use case descriptions which had "inputs/outputs" like an algorithm and a "basic/alternate" structure like a use case. Not surprisingly, with use cases being used to represent algorithms, the model was full of "algorithm use cases" that had a split personality (half algorithm, half use case). The problem here is that the best-practice guidelines for writing good use cases are not the same as the guidelines for describing algorithms. Thus representing algorithms with use cases tends to be confusing to both creators and readers of the model.

While none of this was particularly surprising to us, it struck me right between the eyes that it was time to do something about it, and that the compelling reason to do it now was that resistance to modeling (which didn't need any further ammunition) was being fueled by the fact that the model simply wasn't working (i.e. was not easily understandable) as well as it should.

Modeling Tip: Watch for signs that your software process may need tailoring

Here are some telltale warning signs to look out for:

The arguments against modeling seem compelling

There is inevitably some resistance to any sort of UML modeling. Generally there is a "hardcore" group of disbelievers who think that any sort of pre-coding modeling activity is a waste of time, and some others who understand the need for a more disciplined development approach and will make some attempt at making modeling work. When the "disbelievers" present arguments that seem compelling to a large percentage of the team, and when those who are trying to make modeling work are finding that it's tough sledding, it's a clue that the process needs tailoring.

The model feels like a hindrance rather than a help

The purpose of UML models is not to slow a project down for no good purpose (we realize this may come as a surprise to some). The purpose of the model is to capture all the information that needs to be captured in order for the entire team to develop a common understanding of the problem as completely as possible before coding begins. This enables not just the developers to proceed with their work in a more consistent way, but allows for parallel work by test designers and project management, essential for timely project delivery and managing. For the great majority of systems which involve users and user interfaces, a lot of this information takes the form of use cases. For systems that run with little or no user interaction, use case techniques are not necessarily the most appropriate.

The model is confusing to those who try to read and understand it

A good model should explain the requirements and intended behavior of the system clearly and concisely. If the model is not easy to follow and understand, it may be a sign that tailoring is required.

As Tim and I sat in his office discussing the reasons that we should tailor the process for LSST right now, it was somewhat problematic because Jeff had made it very clear that he didn't think there was enough time to take on any sort of process modifications before PDR. So it was a bit of a dilemma. Finally I suggested to Tim that he and I consider working a small example and showing it to Jeff in the hopes he would agree that it was obviously an improvement. Tim, who you may recall had suggested process tailoring in the first place, agreed. We initially undertook to convert one pipeline (Instrument Signature Removal) into the new format to "try it on for size".

By this time, having had several months to reflect on the problem, I had pretty well formed an idea of how I thought the process should be tailored. I had a precedent for tailoring ICONIX Process for Business Process Modeling where we had used activity diagrams to describe workflows in the ICONIX Business Modeling Roadmap.[28]

This had proven to work pretty well, and the more I looked at the use case diagrams for the LSST pipelines the more convinced I became that there was a fundamental difference between the pipelines, which defined the workflow for a stream of images, and the science algorithms, which perform mathematical operations on the images. I thought the model would be much less confusing if we modeled the workflows on activity diagrams.

Modeling Tip: Guidelines for tailoring a development process

The overriding rule in process tailoring is **"fit the process to the problem"** (and not vice-versa). ICONIX Process uses a core subset of UML diagrams, not because the other parts of UML are never useful, but because this subset has proven to work consistently and effectively while avoiding analysis paralysis on a wide range of projects.

When a project has need for additional UML diagram types, ICONIX Process has always recommended "tailoring up" to include them. If we overzealously stick to the 4 diagram types (class, sequence, use case, and robustness) in the core ICONIX subset, we run the risk of "everything looks like a nail because all we've got is a hammer". In this case the nail is a use case, and the hammer is a use case diagram.

Note that starting from a minimalist modeling subset and tailoring up is a very different approach from that taken by processes such as Rational Unified Process (RUP), which start with everything and require chipping out everything that's not needed. Generally, tailoring down involves a lot more work than tailoring up.

The overriding issue with applying ICONIX Process to the LSST DM software is that ICONIX Process is fundamentally a use-case driven approach to object-oriented design, and the LSST DM software has very few real use cases but is instead heavily algorithm-intensive.

The tailoring I proposed to Tim was actually a pretty simple extension which retained all the benefits[29] of use–case–driven ICONIX Process while being a lot less confusing to everyone

---

[28] www.iconixsw.com/BPRoadmap.html

[29] Another useful principle to follow is: Fix what's broken, but don't try to fix what isn't broken. What wasn't broken about ICONIX Process was using robustness diagrams to identify missing domain objects and identify "controllers" (science algorithms), and using sequence diagrams to do a responsibility-driven allocation of behavior to objects. Jeff,

involved. These changes were:

1) **Don't describe anything other than a real use case with use cases.** Specifically, don't describe workflow as use cases, and don't describe algorithms as use cases. LSST will have "real use cases"; many of these will involve using the data produced by the image processing pipelines. But the part of the software we modeled is almost completely devoid of them.

2) **Describe workflow using activity diagrams.** Essentially, for LSST, this meant that Pipelines and Productions would be described using activity diagrams.

3) **Describe high–level, policy–directed science algorithms on robustness diagrams.** Recognize that "policy" is essentially a proxy for a human sitting in front of a GUI driving the image processing, and treat it as an actor. This allows the robustness diagram rules to be used correctly.

4) **Describe more "atomic" number–crunching science algorithms as controllers on robustness diagrams.** So each controller will specify Inputs, Outputs, Algorithm, and Exceptions.

This tailoring of ICONIX Process is widely applicable beyond LSST to an entire class of algorithm–intensive systems. We present it here as ***ICONIX Process for Algorithm–Intensive Systems*** (or, ***ICONIX Process for Algorithms***).

A Few More Thoughts About ICONIX Process for Algorithms as Used on LSST

Modeling pipelines as activity diagrams involved not only "transmogrifying" the diagram from a use case diagram to an activity diagram, but also incorporating "Policy" as an actor which defined paths through the various pipeline stages. Although the LSST DM software will run without human intervention, various predefined Policies act as proxies for how a human user would guide the software. As it turned out on LSST, there were two parallel sets of image processing pipelines that differed only in the policies to guide them, so making the pipeline activity diagram "policy driven" immediately allowed us to cut the number of "pipeline use case diagrams" in half. This was an encouraging sign as an immediate simplification of the model resulted from the process tailoring we did.

Modeling pipeline stages as high–level algorithms meant replacing the "schizophrenic" algorithm–use case template of:

Tim and I were all unanimously agreed on not sacrificing these benefits. We just needed to find a way to make them work when there were no real use cases.

```
Inputs:
Outputs:
Basic Course:
Alternate Courses:
```

With an activity specification template more suited to algorithms, namely:

```
Inputs:
Outputs:
Algorithm:
Exceptions:
```

Not surprisingly, writing algorithm descriptions as algorithms and not as scenarios made the model much easier to understand. This simple process modification went a long way towards addressing the lack of semantic consistency in the model.

We used robustness diagrams to elaborate activities (is that legal?)[30] The "algorithm–use cases" that had been written in Pasadena had been elaborated on robustness diagrams, and we made the non–standard process enhancement to elaborate the pipeline stage activities with these robustness diagrams as well. Enterprise Architect was flexible enough to support this.

Modeling Tip: Good modeling tools are flexible

I've been bending the rules (and writing new ones) of software development processes for more than 20 years. One of the key attributes that I look for in a tool is *flexibility*. Over the years, I've found that I can make Enterprise Architect do almost anything. It helps me, but doesn't get in my way.

Keeping this elaboration of pipeline stage algorithms on robustness diagrams was important for a number of reasons, one of the primary reasons being that we wanted to maintain the decomposition into "controllers" (lower level algorithms) and "entities" (domain classes). Another important reason was that project estimation tools and techniques relied on the number of controllers within a given pipeline stage (and an estimate of level of effort for each controller) for cost and schedule estimation.

Note that since the domain model had not been consolidated when the original robustness diagrams were created, these diagrams had to be re–visited anyway (since the domain classes appear as "entities" on the robustness diagrams). Not surprisingly, numerous other errors were

---

[30] Luckily I have a license from the UML police to make these sorts of non-standard process enhancements.

uncovered during this cleanup pass through the pipeline stage algorithms. All of this work was absolutely necessary in order to get the project ready for PDR.

Some Final Thoughts on Process Tailoring

While it's generally a good thing to give a process a fair chance to work, and we've found that ICONIX Process "out of the box" works very well for a very wide range of projects, it's also advisable to be alert for any fundamental issues that might require tailoring. In the case of LSST DM, it proved too cumbersome (although not impossible) to bend the rules and model algorithms as use cases.

While we knew from the beginning that we were stretching and twisting the rules during the Pasadena workshop, the team still managed to produce a large amount of useful work. In hindsight it might have been advisable to tailor the process a bit earlier, but, as with many things, the issues became clearer as more progress was made.

The most important conclusion is to not be afraid to tweak the process if it's not working as well as it should. Neither ICONIX Process nor any other software process is chiseled on stone tablets, and they should never be treated as if they were.

If it ain't broke don't fix it, but if it is... don't hesitate to do what's necessary to make your process work for you.

All's Well That Ends Well...

As things turned out, the LSST PDR date was slipped by the funding agencies, allowing time for Tim, with assistance from Robyn and a couple of working sessions with me, to update the entire model in this fashion with excellent results—some of this updating is still in progress as I'm writing this. We'll use the algorithmically tailored version of the model to show how to detect asteroids that might hit the Earth (and other moving objects) in the next chapter.

CHAPTER 5

How Do You Detect an Asteroid That Might Hit the Earth?

This chapter pulls together a few pieces of the LSST model to tell the story of how the LSST software will identify moving objects from its torrent of images.

Domain Model

Let's start with a small fragment from the LSST Domain Model, focusing on "Astronomical Objects" (`AstroObjects`). The domain model, in addition to it's large main "almost everything" diagram, also is organized into subset diagrams showing clusters of related objects. It's often a lot easier to look at the subset diagrams, and that's the case here.

You can see from Figure 5-1 that we've identified a `Solar System Object` as a distinct kind of `AstroObject`, and that `Solar System Object`s have `Orbit`s. We've also identified something mysterious called `Ephemerides`. As it turns out, Ephemerides are important to our story. But... (as I asked Tim on a recent visit to Tucson) what's an Ephemeride?

Here's where Tim having defined his domain objects comes in handy. We can just look it up under E for `Ephemeride`. Using the domain model as a glossary is useful on any project, but when you have a distributed team like LSST, it's absolutely essential (see Figure 5-2).

ICONIX PROCESS FOR ALGORITHM DEVELOPMENT

Name: Domain Model - AstroObject View
Author: Tim Axelrod
Version: 1.0
Created: 12/8/2008 3:25:52 PM
Updated: 5/11/2009 2:59:14 PM

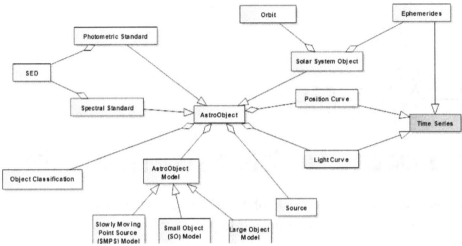

Figure 5-1. Domain model showing different kinds of Astronomical Objects.

3.1.34   Discontinuity Mask

A **Mask** associated with a **CCD**. It has four mask planes: X-, X+, Y-, Y+. If a pixel has the X- plane set, the corresponding **CCD** pixel has a geometrical discontinuity with the pixel in the negative X direction. Similarly for X+ (positive X), Y- (negative Y), and Y+ (positive Y) planes.

3.1.35   ECG List

3.1.36   Electrical Geometry

The **Electrical Geometry** specifies the order in which the **Segment** pixels are read out, including not only the physical imaging pixels, but also the overscan pixels that can be located before and/or after each row of physical pixels.

3.1.37   Ephemerides

A **Time Series** of predicted **Sky Coordinates** for a **Solar System Object.**

3.1.38   Ephemeris Collection

A table of values which gives the positions of astronomical objects at a given time or times.

Figure 5-2. Using the Domain Model as a Project Glossary is a very useful technique.

56

As you can see, an `Ephemeride` is a `Time Series` of predicted `Sky Coordinates` for a `Solar System Object`. In other words, the predicted track of an object in the solar system (like a Martian Spacecraft, or an asteroid that might be heading for Earth, or the planet Neptune, or one of Saturn's moons, or even the Hubble Space Telescope). In the words of an old electromagnetic theory professor of mine, this is "intuitively obvious to the casual observer."

Modeling Tip: It all starts with Domain Modeling

In complex systems like LSST, the Domain Model can become quite large. When this happens, create "subset view" diagrams that show a relate set of objects. Don't forget to define all your domain classes unambiguously.

So far, so good. The LSST Domain Model has an object that exists specifically for the purpose we have in mind. Now let's take a look at how we're going to compute these Ephemerides.

Image Processing Pipelines

LSST's image processing software uses a "pipeline" architecture. Images go in one end of the pipeline through an `Input Queue`, and are analyzed as they pass through various "processing stages", then exit through an Output Queue. LSST's middleware defines a general purpose architecture for pipelines which allows for parallel processing of the image stream. Parallel processing is an absolute necessity when you're dealing with a stream of 3 gigapixel images with a new image coming through every few minutes. We're going to be looking at one of many LSST pipelines later in this chapter, a pipeline called "Day MOPS".

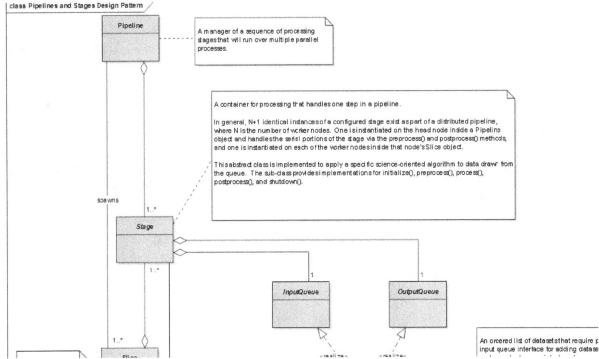

Figure 5-3. LSST's middleware manages the image processing pipelines.

Policies

LSST's software will operate at much too high a rate for there to be human guidance and direction during the execution of a pipeline. However, there are many occasions where human guidance is necessary. LSST pipelines can be controlled by `Policies`, which are sets of parameters that human experts (astrophysicists) can define. So a `Policy` is really like a proxy object that replaces a person who would be guiding the image processing software if you slowed down the processing by a couple of million times (see Figure 5-4).

3.2.2.6.1   Policy

Policy is a container for holding hierarchical configuration data in memory. A policy is a set of named parameters that can be used to configure the internal data and behavior of an object within an application.

An important feature Policy objects is that the parameters can be loaded in from a file. Thus, it allows applications fine-grained control of objects even if much of the configuration parameters they provide are normally set to defaults and otherwise do not change. The Policy interface allows an application to pull out parameter values by name. Typically, the application "knows" the names it needs from a Policy to configure itself--that is, these names and the use of their values are hard-coded into the application. The application simply calls one of the get methods to retrieve a typed value for the parameter. (Nevertheless, if necessary, the parameter names contained in a policy can be retrieved via the \c names( ) member function.)

Figure 5-4. LSST's pipelines are "policy driven". Policy objects are sets of parameters that effectively act as proxies for expert astrophysicists. These parameters guide the image analysis, since the image processing runs far too quickly to allow for actual human intervention.

The Day MOPS Pipeline

Since LSST Pipelines are used to define workflow (and are not really use cases) we're using an activity diagram to describe the workflow, instead of trying to describe the pipeline detail on a use case diagram. So it's clear in the model that when we see an activity diagram, we're working at the upper levels of the model.

Figure 5-5 shows the activity diagram that describes our moving object detection pipeline.

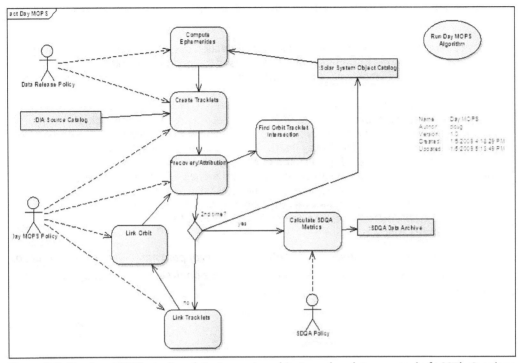

Figure 5-5. The Day MOPS pipeline detects moving objects and updates several of LSST's Catalogs, including the Solar System Object Catalog.

Near Earth Object Detection

LSST's Day MOPS pipeline is being developed in close collaboration with a project called PAN-STARRS[31] (Panoramic Survey Telescope & Rapid Response System). The PAN-STARRS website has an interesting discussion about Near Earth Object (NEO) detection and the potential threat from asteroids.[32]

Also, NASA JPL maintains a Near Earth Object website if you'd like to take a peek at which asteroids will be making close passes to us in the near future[33]. The PAN-STARRS website lists their digital cameras as the world's largest, at 1.4 gigapixels[34]; this won't be true anymore after LSST's 3.2 gigapixel (that's 3200 megapixels)[35] camera gets built.

---

[31] http://pan-starrs.ifa.hawaii.edu/public/

[32] http://pan-starrs.ifa.hawaii.edu/public/asteroid-threat/asteroid_threat.html

[33] http://neo.jpl.nasa.gov/

[34] http://pan-starrs.ifa.hawaii.edu/public/design-features/cameras.html

[35] www.lsst.org/lsst/gallery/camera/suzanne

A Look Inside the Pipeline Stages

Within each activity, we're elaborating the processing on a robustness diagram as if the activity were a use case, and we're representing Policy as an actor, and (to make our robustness diagram rules work correctly) defining Policy Readers as boundary objects. Since the robustness diagram is a conceptual design diagram, it doesn't really matter whether a policy reader object will ever be implemented. We're using it in the model as a device to help us identify what the different policy parameters should be.

Modeling Tip: Robustness diagrams help "Object Discovery"

Robustness diagrams (aka "Martian") are conceptual design diagrams that are useful to help you discover details about your object model. Since it's not an implementation model, it's OK to add conceptual objects like `Policy Readers` to help us discover what data we're reading from the `Policy`.

See Figure 5-6 for an example of a robustness diagram.

By elaborating pipeline stages within activities, and allowing for "controllers" (lower level algorithms) within the robustness diagram, we're putting a limit on how many levels of "algorithms within algorithms within algorithms within algorithms" we're going to show in the model. The controllers that are connected to the Policy Readers help us to identify exactly what needs to go into the Policy.

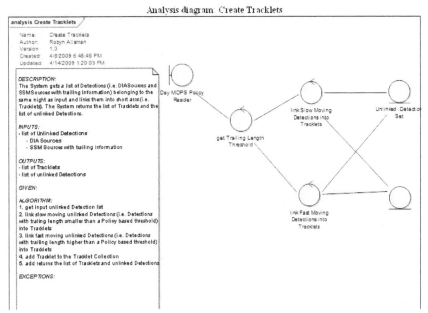

Figure 5-6. A robustness diagram for Tracklet Creation. "Martian" notation is actually pretty simple.

Notice that even though we're using it to describe a policy–directed algorithm instead of a use case, the robustness diagram still works. This allows us to leverage other capabilities of ICONIX Process and the Sparx Agile/ICONIX add–in to generate skeleton sequence diagrams and test cases automatically.

Modeling Tip: Use ICONIX/Algorithms to retain all the benefits of ICONIX Process

The standard, use-case-driven, ICONIX Process discovers details about an object model using robustness analysis, and does a responsibility-driven allocation of behavior using sequence diagrams. Additionally, the Agile/ICONIX add-in from Sparx Systems supports automatic generation of test cases and JUnit/NUnit test code from robustness and sequence diagrams. ICONIX Process for Algorithms retains all of these benefits.

ICONIX Process for Algorithms is useful for a wide range of algorithm-intensive systems.

Figure 5-7 shows an algorithm for a pipeline stage that hasn't been elaborated (yet) on a robustness diagram. Exactly as with use–case–driven ICONIX Process, drawing the robustness diagram helps us discover additional domain objects that may still be missing from the model. So our process tailoring has retained the benefits of use–case–driven ICONIX Process, without trying to force-fit algorithms into use cases.

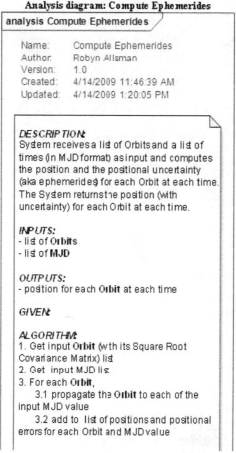

Figure 5-7. This algorithm for computing Ephemerides will soon be detailed on a robustness diagram.

Converging Towards a Solution

You can see the benefits of a forward-modeling and reverse-engineering approach here, with a reverse-engineered database schema for MOPS (see Figure 5-8). By using LSST's R&D Phase for both modeling and prototyping different areas of functionality, the project minimizes risk. When LSST reaches the Construction phase, there will be very little doubt of a successful outcome.

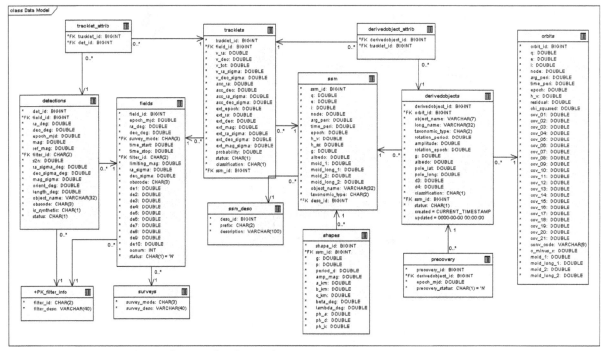

Figure 5-8. Reverse-engineered MOPS database schema.

Modeling Tip: Modeling + Reverse Engineering minimizes risk

Once again, you can see how the capabilities of the modeling tool (in this case, EA's ability to reverse-engineer database schemas in addition to a wide range of programming languages) allows for a risk-mitigation strategy that's crucial for a project of the complexity of LSST.

Conclusion

Detecting asteroids which might impact the Earth is a small, but important, portion of LSST's overall science mission. Hopefully, you've been able to follow the discussion presented in this chapter that explains how this capability will be provided by the Day MOPS image processing pipeline. If you have, that's a good sign that our tailoring of ICONIX Process has resulted in a UML model that successfully and unambiguously explains the design of the LSST software.

R O A D M A P # 2

ICONIX PROCESS FOR EMBEDDED SYSTEMS

Embedded Systems Development With SysML—An Illustrated Example Using Enterprise Architect

by Doug Rosenberg with Sam Mancarella

PROLOGUE

Back to the Future

This book represents a departure from what I've been doing at ICONIX over the last 25 years, which has been focused mainly on Software Engineering, but a book on how to develop real-time embedded systems is actually a "return to my roots" in Electrical Engineering.

My degree is actually in EE, not Computer Science, and my path to being involved with Software Engineering had its formative years when I was working as a programmer in Computer Aided Design for VLSI in the aerospace industry in southern California, and also up in Silicon Valley. So even though SysML is a new area for me, I'm inherently familiar with the problems that SysML helps to solve.

My first four jobs out of college (in the early 1980s) were involved with VLSI design. Three of these (two at TRW and one at Hughes Research Labs) were on a project called VHSIC (Very High Speed Integrated Circuits), which is what the "V" in VHDL stands for. At TRW my work involved extending some of the early "design rule checking" software to cover more a complex fabrication process that allowed us to deliver gigahertz-level speeds, which was much more of an accomplishment 30 years ago than it is today. I also worked a bit with SPICE, one of the earliest "circuit simulators" (more about simulation in the "SysML parametrics" discussion in Chapter 5).

Later, after a short stint up in Silicon Valley working on something called "symbolic layout and compaction" at a company called Calma, I returned to TRW where I designed and programmed an application called "Hierarchical Layout Verification" which recursively decomposed a complete integrated circuit layout into sub-cells (now called "blocks" in SysML), determined their input and output "ports" (another familiar SysML concept), and checked both physical design rules and electrical connectivity.

During this time, my boss Jim Peterson at TRW was developing one of the early Hardware

Description Languages, which he called THDL (for TRW Hardware Description Language). THDL itself was an extension of CIF (Caltech Intermediate Format[36]) which had been developed in Carver Mead"s research group when Jim was a grad student at Caltech. Since Jim"s THDL work was funded under the VHSIC contract it's a safe bet that some of the concepts in VHDL had their roots in THDL.

After my second go-round at TRW, I went to work at Hughes Research Labs in Malibu, CA, developing the interface from CAD systems (most notably Calma, who owned about 80% of the market back then) to something called the VHSIC Electron Beam Lithography System. This was another ambitious project that pushed the state of the art in fabrication technology far ahead of what it had been previously. We were writing one-tenth-of-a-micron lines on silicon wafers using electron beams (still not bad today) back in 1984.

When Sparx Systems asked me to write this eBook, I discovered a kindred spirit in Sam Mancarella, who is largely responsible for a great deal of the implementation of Enterprise Architect's SysML solution. Sam also developed the Audio Player example that this book is written around, which is such a complete and comprehensive example that it made my writing task very easy. I want to make it completely clear that Sam deserves ALL of the credit for developing this example, and that my contribution to this project was simply writing the manuscript around the example. My electrical engineering background made it obvious to me how good Sam"s example is, and allowed me to see how the pieces fit together.

---

[36] Introduction to VHDL By R. D. M. Hunter, T. T. Johnson, p.17-18

CHAPTER 1

An Introduction to SysML and Enterprise Architect Engineering Edition

A Roadmap for Embedded System Development

It's easy for a book to present a taxonomy of disjointed SysML diagrams and then leave you to figure out how to combine those diagrams into a meaningful model. In fact, that's what the majority of SysML books that we've seen appear to do. But with this book, we're going to introduce you to SysML and the Systems Engineering Edition of Enterprise Architect in a rather different way.

At ICONIX, we've had pretty good success when we defined an unambiguous development process, and presented that development process in "roadmap" form. We've developed process roadmaps for use case driven software development, business modeling, design driven testing, and algorithm-intensive software design. In this book we're going to do it again, this time for embedded systems that involve a combination of hardware and software. We'll explain the roadmap at the high level in this chapter, and then each of the following chapters will detail one of the high-level activities on the top-level roadmap. Along the way, We'll show you how Enterprise Architect's System Engineering Edition supports the process we're describing, while illustrating each step of the process by example.

In addition to providing complete support for all SysML 1.1 diagrams, the Enterprise Architect Systems Engineering edition combines advanced features such as executable code generation from UML models (including support for hardware languages such as Verilog and VHDL),

executable SysML Parametric diagrams and advanced scripting. We'll explore this unique combination of advanced capabilities in the last half of this book.

Specifically,

• In Chapter 5 we'll explore Enterprise Architect's SysML Simulation Support, which provides the capability of simulating SysML 1.1 constraint models with results graphing capabilities

• In Chapter 6 We'll describe support for Hardware Description Languages, including Verilog, VHDL and SystemC, with support for generating State Machine code

• In Chapter 7 We'll illustrate Enterprise Architect's support for generating functional source code for State Machines, Interactions and Activities in C, C++, C#, Java and VB.Net

Each of these capabilities, taken standalone, adds a significant amount of "horsepower" for a systems engineering effort. We'll show you how to combine these capabilities into a single process roadmap that's greater than the sum of its parts.

Figure 1-1 shows the top level roadmap for ICONIX Process for Embedded Systems. As you can see, our roadmap starts off by defining requirements, proceeds through modeling of system behavior and block structure, and then through definition of constraints and parametrics, simulation, and then implementation in both hardware and software. We'll take you through each of these activities at a summary level in this chapter, and then in more detail, illustrated by a comprehensive Audio Player example, in Chapters 2 to 7.

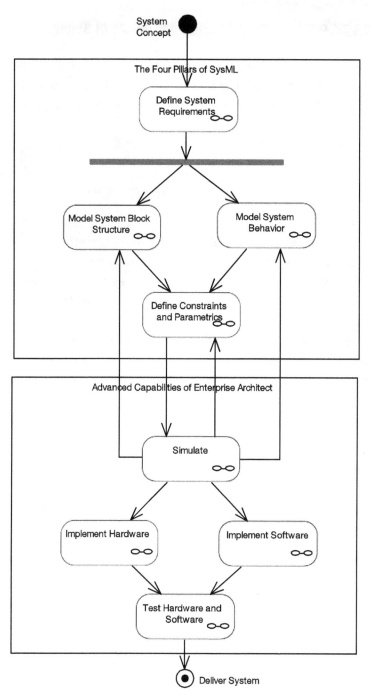

Figure 1-1. ICONIX Process Roadmap for Embedded Systems Development

Requirements, Structure, Behavior, and Parametrics—the Four Pillars of SysML

Our Embedded System Development Process Roadmap is organized around producing a SysML model that is generally organized into four sections. These parts of the overall system model (Requirements, Structure, Behavior, and Parametrics) are sometimes referred to as "The Four Pillars of SysML".[37]

Requirements

Requirements are generally categorized as Functional Requirements, which represent capabilities of a system, and Non-Functional Requirements, which cover such areas as Performance and Reliability. You can organize Requirements into hierarchies on requirement diagrams. Enterprise Architect supports allocation of requirements to other elements using a simple drag-and-drop, and automatic generation of traceability matrices.

Figure 1-2 shows the steps for Requirements definition from our process roadmap. Note that allocation of Requirements to System Elements is really an ongoing process as the model is developed, and largely occurs within other roadmap activities. We'll explore Requirements Definition in more detail in Chapter 2.

---

[37] OMG Systems Modeling Language Tutorial, INCOSE 2008

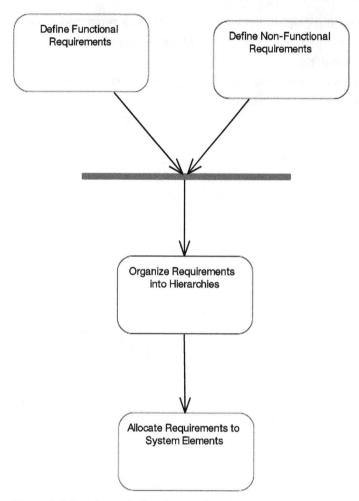

Figure 1-2. Roadmap: Define System Requirements

Structure

Blocks can be used to represent hardware, software, or just about anything else. Block definition diagrams represent system structure. Internal block diagrams describe the internals of a block such as parts, ports, and connectors. As with UML, Packages are used to organize the model.

If you think of a Block as an electronic circuit (one of many things that a Block can describe), the Ports define the input and output signals to/from the circuit. SysML allows you to describe the input signals and transformations in great detail, and Enterprise Architect contains a built-in simulator that allows you to plot the output graphically or export to a comma-separated value file. You'll see how this works in detail in Chapter 5. Defining the Block structure is a prerequisite for defining parametrics and running simulations.

Figure 1-3 shows how our process roadmap approaches defining system structure. See Chapter 3 for an expanded discussion on modeling structure.

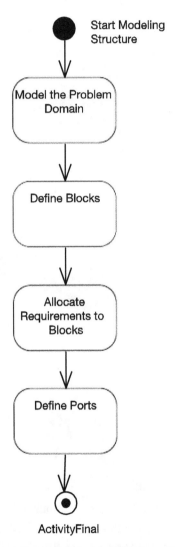

Figure 1-3. Roadmap: Model System Block Structure

Behavior

SysML provides four main constructs to represent different aspects of system behavior: use cases, activity diagrams, sequence diagrams, and state machines.

Our roadmap (see Figure 1-4) shows two parallel branches for modeling system behavior.

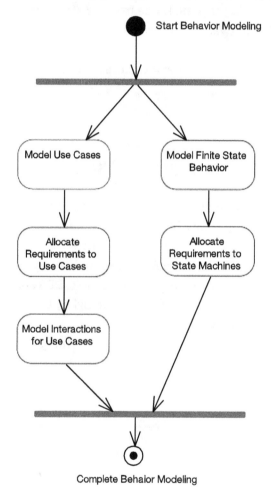

Figure 1-4. Roadmap: Model System Behavior

One branch starts with use cases,[38] which describe scenarios of how users will interact with the system. Use cases generally consist of a "sunny-day" part which describes a typical success

---

[38] See "Use Case Driven Object Modeling with UML: Theory and Practice" by Doug Rosenberg and Matt Stephens for a lot more information about use cases.

path for the scenario, and multiple "rainy-day" parts which describe unusual conditions, exceptions, failures, etc. Use cases are typically detailed on Interaction (Sequence) Diagrams.

The other branch on the roadmap involves defining event-driven, finite-state behavior of some part of a system using state machines. As a simple example, there is finite state behavior associated with the power charging circuitry on our Audio Player. One of Enterprise Architect's unique capabilities is the ability to generate functional (algorithmic) code from state machines. As You'll see, these state machines can be realized in software or in hardware using Hardware Description Languages (HDLs).

Requirements are allocated to both use cases and states. Chapter 4 explores behavior modeling in detail.

Advanced Features of the Enterprise Architect System Engineering Edition

Enterprise Architect Systems Engineering edition contains a number of unique features for systems and software engineers working on embedded systems. The Systems Engineering edition combines new features such as executable SysML Parametric diagrams and advanced scripting with executable code generation from UML models (including support for hardware languages such as Verilog and VHDL, and bundles licenses for DoDAF-MODAF, SysML, DDS and IDE integration products to provide powerful model-driven construction tools to tightly bind your code development in Eclipse or Visual Studio with the UML/SysML.

Our process roadmap (see Figure 1-5) leverages these unique capabilities into a synergistic development process.

Start defining constraints and parametrics

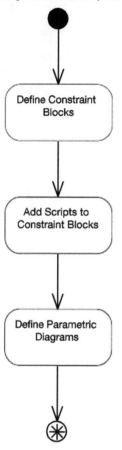

Simulate Parametric Models

Figure 1-5. Roadmap: Define Constraints and Parametrics

Parametrics

Parametrics allow us to define detailed characteristics, physical laws, and constraints on system blocks that allow us to simulate how a system will behave, then make engineering tradeoffs, and re-simulate until our design meets the specified requirements.

Our roadmap (see Figure 1-6) provides two high-level activities in this area; the first to define constraint blocks and parametric diagrams, and the second to configure and execute the simulations.

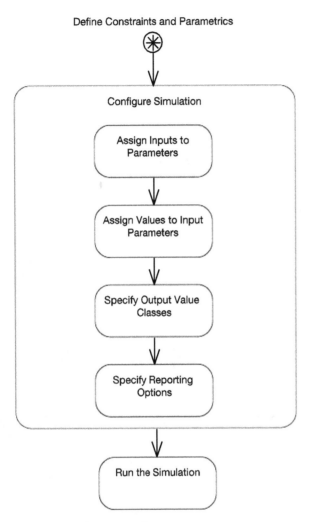

Figure 1-6. Roadmap: Simulate

The ability to configure and execute simulations within Enterprise Architect, eliminating the need to export the model to external simulation software, is one of the unique capabilities of the Sparx SysML solution.

Enterprise Architect's built-in support for scripting and graphical display of simulation results tightens the feedback loop on making engineering tradeoffs in the model to rapidly ensure that all system requirements are met. You'll see how this works in detail in Chapter 5.

Implement Hardware

Hardware Description Languages allow the specification of electronic circuits in a software-like representation. According to Wikipedia:

> In electronics, a hardware description language or HDL is any language from a class of computer languages and/or programming languages for formal description of electronic circuits, and more specifically, digital logic. It can describe the circuit's operation, its design and organization, and tests to verify its operation by means of simulation.
>
> HDLs are standard text-based expressions of the spatial and temporal structure and behaviour of electronic systems. Like concurrent programming languages, HDL syntax and semantics includes explicit notations for expressing concurrency. However, in contrast to most software programming languages, HDLs also include an explicit notion of time, which is a primary attribute of hardware. Languages whose only characteristic is to express circuit connectivity between a hierarchy of blocks are properly classified as netlist languages used on electric computer-aided design (CAD).
>
> HDLs are used to write executable specifications of some piece of hardware. A simulation program, designed to implement the underlying semantics of the language statements, coupled with simulating the progress of time, provides the hardware designer with the ability to model a piece of hardware before it is created physically. It is this executability that gives HDLs the illusion of being programming languages. Simulators capable of supporting discrete-event (digital) and continuous-time (analog) modeling exist, and HDLs targeted for each are available.[39]

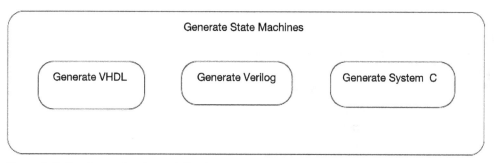

Figure 1-7. Roadmap: Implement Hardware

---

[39] http://en.wikipedia.org/wiki/Hardware_description_languages

Enterprise Architect's long-proven ability to generate code has been extended to support code generation in VHDL, Verilog, and System C in the Systems Engineering Edition. While code generation is independent of SysML usage, from a process roadmap standpoint, this means we can drive both hardware and software implementation from our SysML model. Once code is generated in an HDL, It's possible to "compile to silicon" to realize the hardware solution on a chip.

We'll explore hardware implementation in Chapter 6.

Implement Software

Software implementations can leverage a variety of powerful capabilities that are included with the System Engineering Edition of Enterprise Architect. Two of the more important and unique capabilities are:

• The ability to generate functional (algorithmic) code from behavioral models (state machines, activity diagrams, and interaction diagrams)

• The ability to integrate Enterprise Architect models into development environments such as Eclipse and Visual Studio.

Figure 1-8 provides a high-level look at the Software Implementation activity from the roadmap.

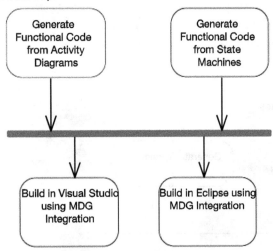

Figure 1-8. Implement Software

We'll explore these unique capabilities and how they work together in Chapter 7.

Introducing the Audio Player Example

Over the course of this book, We'll be illustrating the steps in our process by presenting diagrams from an example project. Our example (developed by Sam Mancarella) will be a hardware/software system that most everyone is familiar with—an Audio Player.

The top level Package Diagram in Figure 1-9 shows how the example model is organized.

Requirements Model
This package contains the models that define the requirements of the Portable Audio Player. The model contains requirement specifications, use cases, interactions, state machines and constraint blocks.

Specifications
+ Durability
+ Media Access
+ Performance
+ User Friendliness

Specifications

Use Cases
+ Top Level
+ Maintain Audio Player
+ Maintain Playlist
+ Operate Audio Player

Use Cases

Constraint Blocks
+ EchoDSP

Constraint Blocks

Interactions
+ Operate Audio Player
+ Maintain Playlist
+ Maintain Audio Player
+ deviceInContext
+ listener

Interactions

State Machines
+ DSP Effects
+ Operating States
+ Playlist Maintenance

State Machines

Figure 1-9. SysML models are organized into Requirements, Behavior, Structure, Constraints and Parametrics, and include both Hardware and Software Implementation models.

You'll become intimately familiar with Sam's audio player example, as we'll be using it to illustrate the various activities on our roadmap throughout the following chapters.

CHAPTER 2

Audio Player Requirements

Requirements Roadmap

Requirements are the foundation of a SysML model. The purpose of the system that you're modeling is to satisfy the requirements. So, as you"d expect, the roadmap begins with defining requirements (see Figure 2-1).

As you saw in Chapter 1, Requirements are usually classified as Functional (e.g. Requirements that represent specific system features or capabilities), and Non-Functional (e.g. Requirements that don't apply to specific features such as ease-of-use). It's important to organize these Requirements effectively, otherwise the Requirements model can become Dysfunctional.[40]

When you think about Requirements in a SysML model, you're considering Hardware Requirements, Software Requirements, and Requirements that relate to the Environment that your system will interact with. For example, our Audio Player will interact with its operating environment, which includes "listening conditions" (noise, weather), and the clothing of the listener.

---

[40] For more on avoiding Dysfunctional Requirements, see *Use Case Driven Object Modeling with UML – Theory and Practice*, by Doug Rosenberg and Matt Stephens.

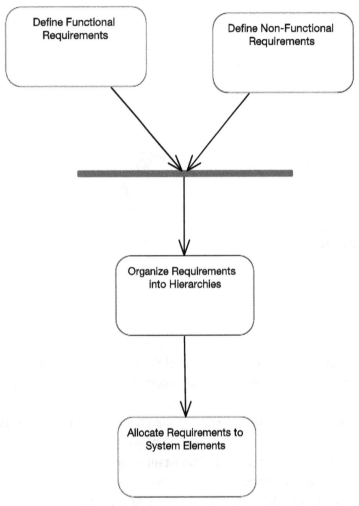

Figure 2-1. Requirements Definition Roadmap

These domain aspects drive downstream requirements which describe items such as shock resistance, waterproofing etc., because we expect the audio player to operate within the listeningDomain defined by this (ibd) block diagram which describes the listeningConditions to which the player will be subjected.

The "blocks" shown in Figure 2-2 will be decomposed into their parts to describe this domain system.

Modeling Tip: It's easy to import graphics into Enterprise Architect Models

As you can see from the example in Figure 2-2, adding some graphics (photos, illustrations, etc) to a model can make it far easier to understand. Enterprise Architect makes this easy to do. There are several ways to do this, but one of the easiest is to copy an image to the clipboard, then right-click an element on a diagram, select Appearance from the context menu, and then select Apply Image from Clipboard. It only takes a few seconds, but adds a lot to the readability of your model.

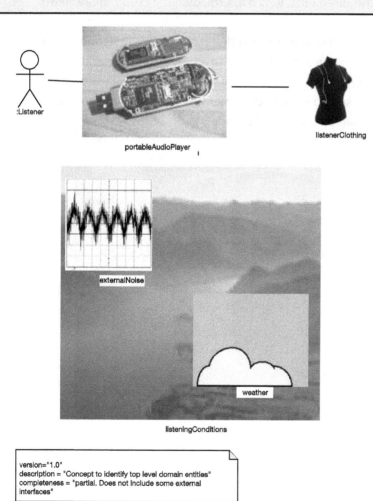

Figure 2-2. SysML Models include Hardware, Software, and the Environment within which a system must operate.

Audio Player Requirements

SysML defines seven relationships between Requirements. These fall into two categories: relationships between Requirements, which include containment, derive, and copy; and relationships between requirements and other model elements, which include satisfy, verify, refine, and trace.

The crosshair notation in the Audio Player Requirements diagram in Figure 2-3 shows the use of containment to organize requirements hierarchically into Categories meaning that the Specifications Package *owns* the requirements, which in turn, own the "sub requirements" beneath.

Enterprise Architect has a couple of built-in features that make it easy to define which requirements are satisfied by which model elements, and to automatically generate a relationship matrix to show these relationships (see Figures 2-4 and 2-5).

In the upcoming chapters, you'll see how the Requirements we've identified here are satisfied by various aspects of the Audio Player SysML model.

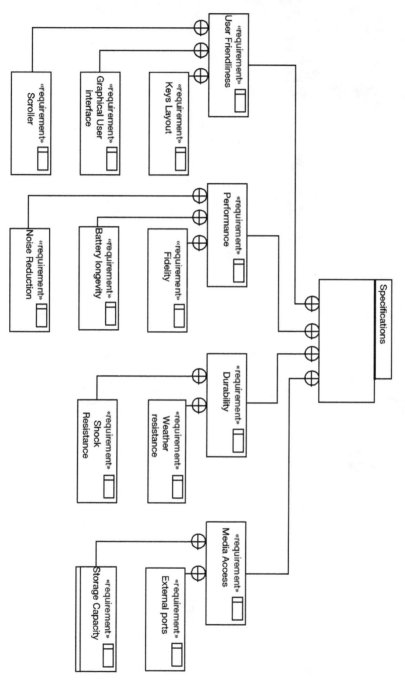

Figure 2-3. Requirements for our Audio Player are organized into Categories such as User Friendliness, Performance and Durability.

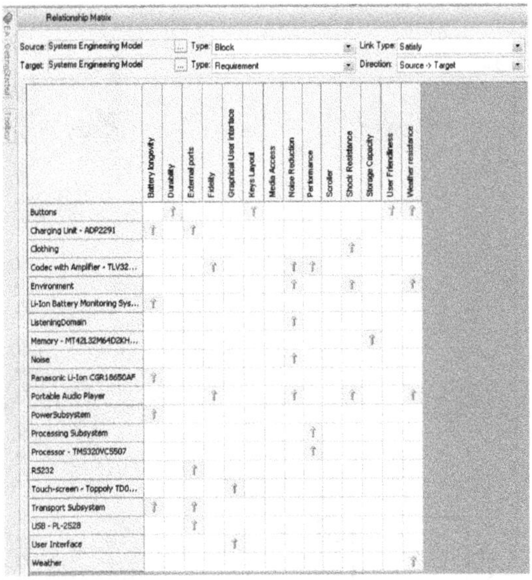

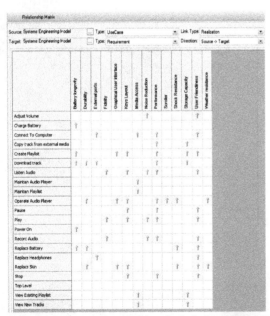

Figure 2-4. Enterprise Architect's Relationship Matrix makes it easy to see the allocation of Requirements to Blocks

![Relationship Matrix screenshot for Use Cases]

Figure 2-5. Enterprise Architect's Relationship Matrix makes it easy to see the allocation of Requirements to Use Cases

CHAPTER 3

Audio Player Behavior

Behavior Modeling Roadmap

Behavior Modeling describes the dynamic behavior of the System as it interacts with users and with the environment. You'll use interaction diagrams and use cases to model interactions between users and the system, and state machines to describe event-driven behavior that's not user-centric. Figure 3-1 shows the Roadmap activities.

As you can see, you approach behavior modeling in two parallel branches, one for use cases and the other for state machines. Each branch includes allocation of Requirements to model elements (use cases or states). Use cases are described in natural language at the high level, and are detailed on interaction (sequence) diagrams.

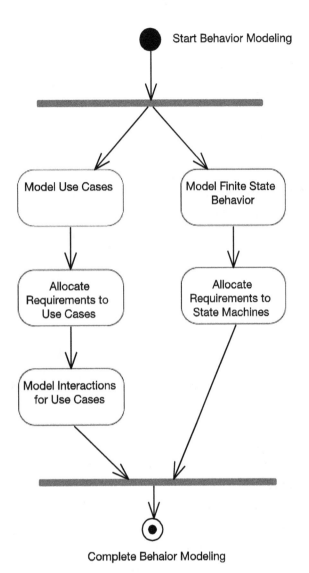

Start Behavior Modeling

Complete Behaior Modeling

Figure 3-1. Behavior Modeling Roadmap

We'll follow the roadmap through the remainder of this chapter by exploring the dynamic behavior of our Audio Player example. Then in Chapter 4 we'll explore the system structure that supports the desired behavior. We use the terms "static" and "dynamic" to describe the structural and behavioral parts of the model; structure is static in that it doesn"t change once It's defined, while behavior is dynamic—changing based on user actions or external events.

Audio Player Behavior Model

Here we can see the two branches of the dynamic model for our Audio Player. User-centric scenarios, such as Operating the Audio Player, are modeled with use cases, while we can model the Operating States of the device with state machines. Note that Playlist Maintenance has a use case description and is also described using a state machine. Whatever diagrams help to tell the story can be used.

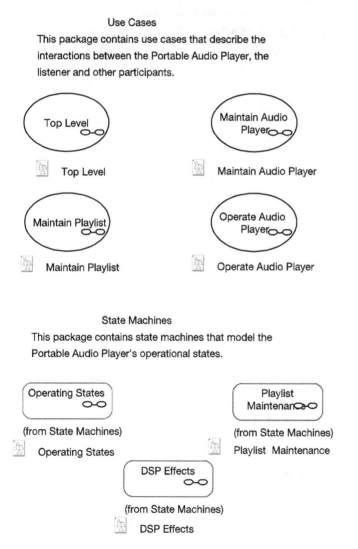

Figure 3-2. Behavioral models include Use Cases, Interactions, and State Machines

Modeling Tip—Models should tell a story

A model's primary purpose is to serve as a communication vehicle to promote a shared understanding about the system being modeled between stakeholders, end-users, analysts, designers, software and hardware engineers, and quality assurance personnel.

Always optimize models for readability, and make sure you "tell the story" clearly and unambiguously.

Figure 3-3 shows the Top Level use cases for the Audio Player. The "eyeglass" icon on the use case bubbles indicate that a child diagram exists, showing more detail about the use case.

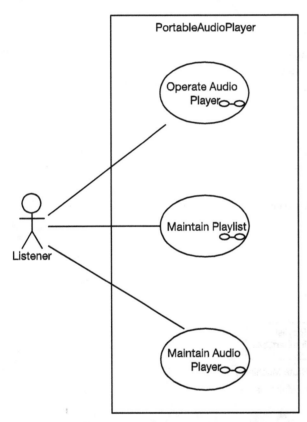

Figure 3-3. Audio Player Top Level Use Cases

Enterprise Architect makes it easy to "drill down" to a child diagram for composite elements. Figure 3-4 shows a child use case diagram for audio player maintenance.

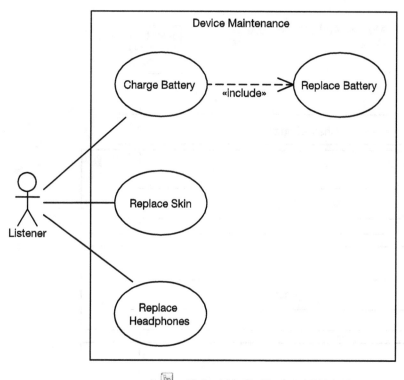

Figure 3-4. Use cases for maintaining the audio player hardware include charging and replacing the battery, and replacing the skin and the headphones.

Enterprise Architect supports "diagram references" for hyperlinking one diagram to another. You can see the reference to the interaction diagram (Figure 3-5) on Figure 3-4, and a link back to the use case view on that diagram.

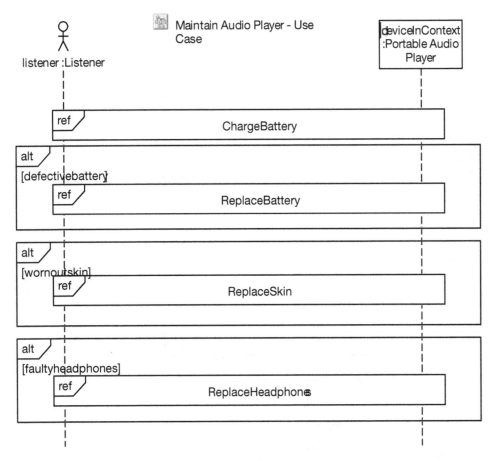

Figure 3-5. The interaction diagram for maintaining the audio player shows 3 alternate courses of action (defective batteries, worn out skin, and faulty headphones) and one normal course (charging the battery).

Figure 3-6 shows the use cases for the basic operations of the Audio Player.

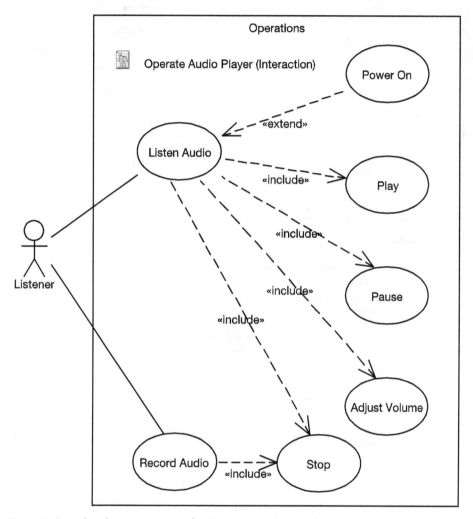

Figure 3-6. Audio Player Use Cases for Listening and Recording

As in the Maintenance use cases, the use case diagram and interaction diagram (Figure 3-7) are cross-linked using Enterprise Architect diagram references. This diagram shows that the Idle, Play, Pause, and Adjust Volume paths can all be performed in parallel.

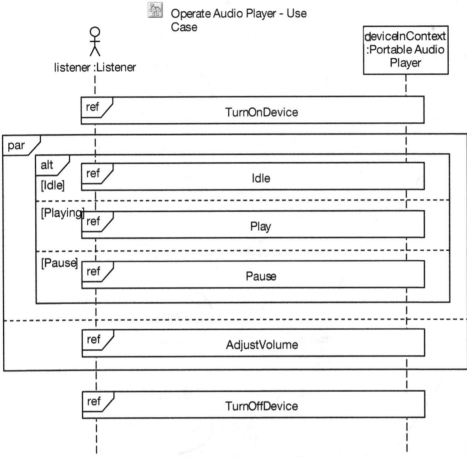

Figure 3-7. Audio Player Interaction diagram for Listening/Recording

Use cases describe how a user interacts with the system. In the next section, you'll see how to describe event-driven behavior using state machines.

Audio Player State Model

For embedded systems, it's often advantageous to describe behavior in terms of operating states, triggering events and system actions. SysML (identically to UML) uses state charts to describe these finite state aspects of a system.

State charts allow nesting of substates on a single diagram. Figure 3-8 shows the detailed behavior of the "On" state of the audio player on the same diagram that shows the "On/Off" behavior. To allocate Requirements to states, simply drag the Requirement from the Enterprise Architect Project Browser and drop it onto the state bubble.

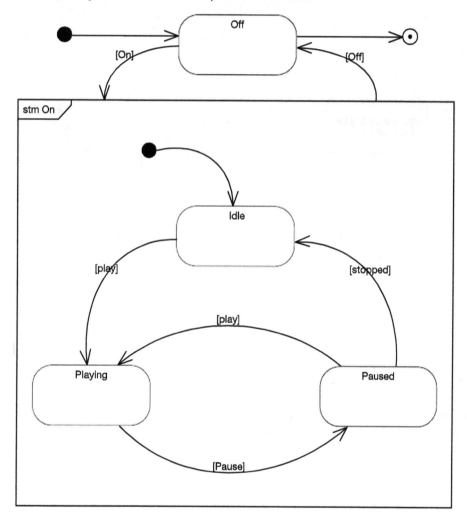

Figure 3-8. Audio Player Operating States

State machines relate operating states of a system (or block) to triggering events such as pressing a button. Figure 3-9 shows how toggling the "Audio EQ" button causes the system to cycle between various audio effects.

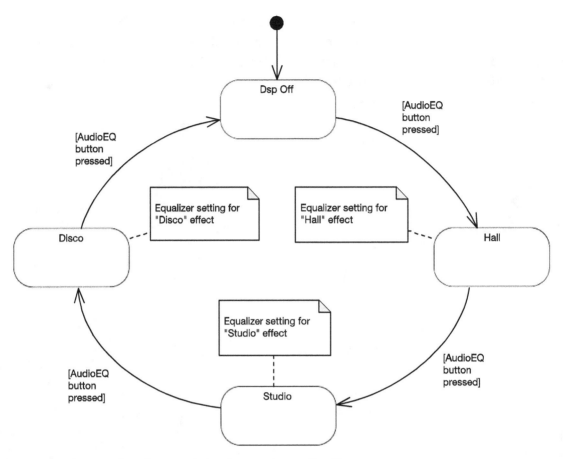

Figure 3-9. State Machine for Digital Signal Processing Audio Effects

There's no absolute rule for choosing when to "tell the story" with use cases and when to use state diagrams. The best guideline is to simply use whichever diagram that tells the story best. Sometimes, the best choice is to use both.

Combining Use Cases and State Machines

Here's an example that shows how use cases, interaction diagrams, and state machines can all be used to describe different aspects of how our audio player system operates.

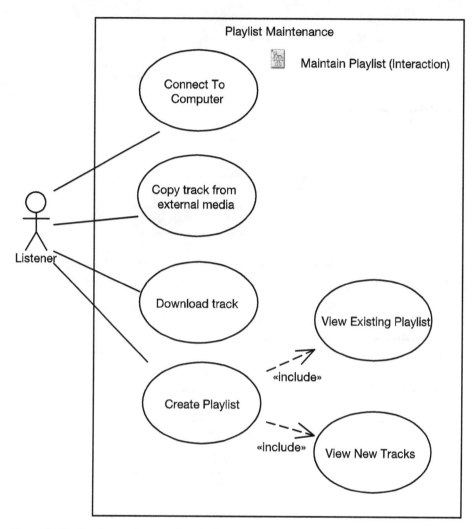

Figure 3-10. Use Case Diagram for Playlist Maintenance

Each diagram provides a different perspective on the system we're modeling. We can use as many views as necessary to "tell the story" so that there are no misunderstandings as we progress from defining Requirements through hardware and software development. Figure 3-11 shows the various scenarios for maintaining playlists, while Figure 3-12 takes a more event-driven perspective.

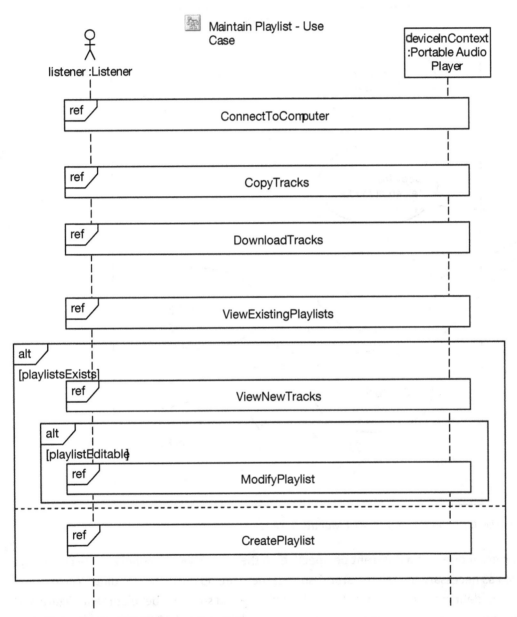

Figure 3-11—Scenarios for maintaining playlists

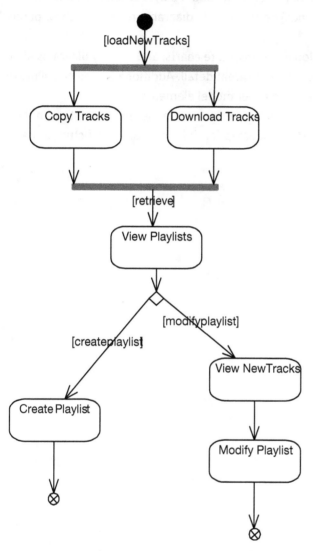

[loadNewTracks]

Copy Tracks

Download Tracks

[retrieve]

View Playlists

[modifyplaylist]

[createplaylist]

View NewTracks

Create Playlist

Modify Playlist

Figure 3-12—State/Event behavior for Playlist maintenance

Note that in order to Modify a Playlist, the Playlist must already exist and be editable. However, tracks may be downloaded and copied independently of those conditions.

The state machine shown in Figure 3-12 provides a different perspective. The top level state machine shows how the behavior depends on connecting/disconnecting the audio player to/from the music server. As you can see, all of the real behavior of maintaining playlists happens when the device is connected.

An activity diagram is used to detail the behavior of the audio player when it's connected. Forks and joins (the solid black horizontal lines) on the activity diagram are used to show parallel paths.

The combination of use cases, interaction diagrams, state charts, and activity diagrams allow you to specify the dynamic behavior of the system in great detail. Additionally, you can allocate Requirements to use cases, states, activities, and other model elements.

This wraps up our discussion of Behavior Modeling, as we've completed all the steps in the Roadmap. In the next chapter we'll explore the Roadmap for defining system structure using blocks.

CHAPTER 4

Audio Player Structure

Now that you've looked at Requirements and Behavior Modeling, it's time to explore how you can use SysML and Enterprise Architect to describe the **structure** of a system. As usual, we'll illustrate by describing the structure of our Audio Player example.

Roadmap: Define Structure

Figure 4-1 shows our Roadmap for modeling Structure.

In SysML, the Block is the primary unit used to describe Structure. Blocks can represent hardware or software elements. Blocks can have Ports, which represent the inputs to, and outputs from, the Block.

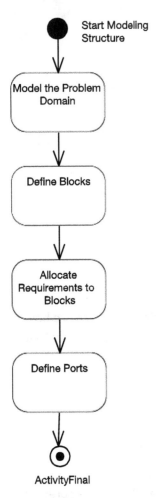

Figure 4-1. Roadmap: Model Structure

Modeling the Problem Domain

Our Structural Modeling roadmap starts with a familiar step to anyone who has seen ICONIX Process for Software-or Business-Domain Modeling. When you build a domain model, you define a set of abstractions based upon things in the real world. Figure 4-2 shows a domain model for our Audio Player. As you can see, the domain model can include real-world elements that are external to our system, such as Clothing and the surrounding Environment.

The purpose of the Problem Domain model is to describe the System in which our Audio

Player will operate under. It's a "system" model used to describe the "context" of our device design—from Requirements through to implementation.

Figure 4-2 shows which systems will interact together with our audio player in a concept known as a System of Systems design.

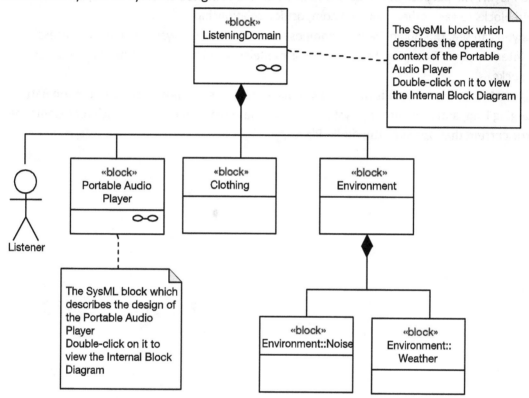

Figure 4-2. Audio Player Domain Model

The "black/filled diamond" association in Figure 2 represents a composition relationship, indicating (for example) that the Environment is "composed of" Noise and Weather.

There are two levels of Block diagramming in SysML: Block Definition Diagrams (BDDs), and Internal Block Diagrams (IBDs). We'll explore these in order in the next few sections of this chapter.

Modeling Block Structure (Block Definition Diagrams)

Figure 4-3 shows the "child" block definition diagram that details the high-level structure of our Audio Player. The purpose of the BDD is to describe the composition of a block by relating nested blocks to each other using the composition relationship.

As you can see, the Audio Player is composed of four main subsystems; Power, Processing, User Interface, and Transport. Each of these is modeled as a block and further decomposed into sub-blocks.

Figure 4-4 shows the details of the Power Subsystem. It's composed of a Lithium-Ion Battery, a Charging Unit, and a Monitoring System. Each of these blocks has a port which represents the electric current that operates the Audio Player.

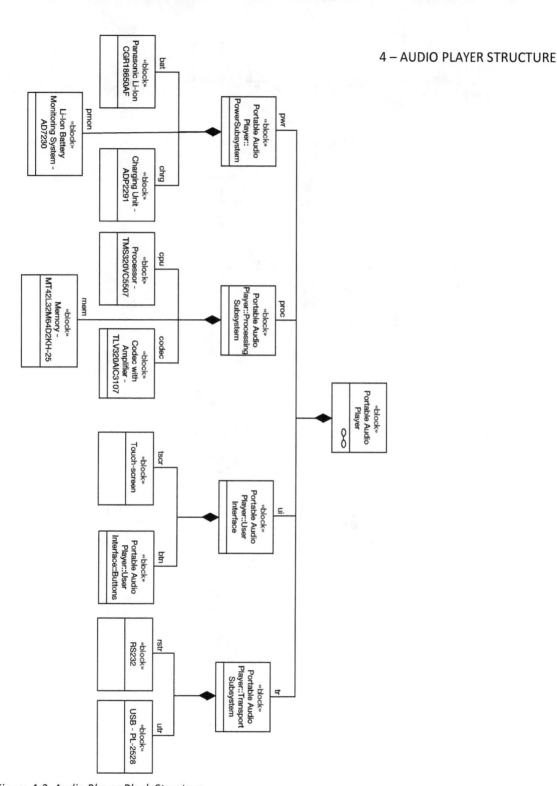

Figure 4-3. Audio Player Block Structure

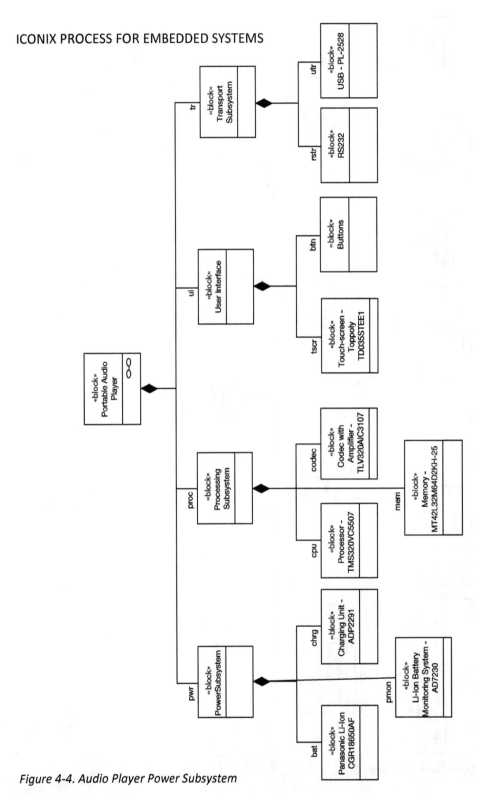

Figure 4-4. Audio Player Power Subsystem

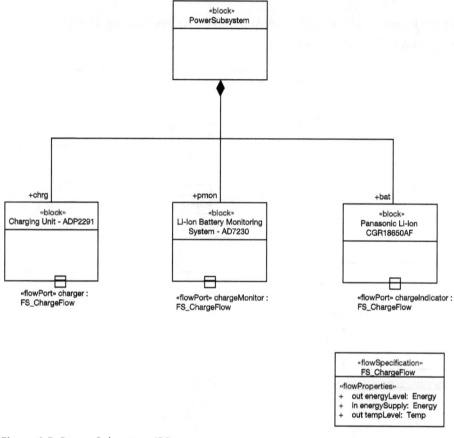

Figure 4-5. Power Subsystem IBD

The Internal Block Diagram specifies the connection of Parts within a Block. As you can see in Figure 4-6, It's possible to show multiple levels of nesting on a single IBD.

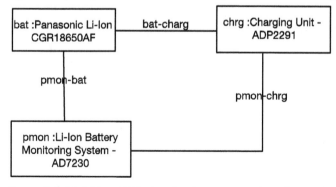

Figure 4-6. Multi-level IBD showing interconnection of parts for the Audio Player

Figure 4-7 shows the internals of the Processing Subsystem. As you can see, the CPU connects to a Memory Unit and a Codec/Amplifier.

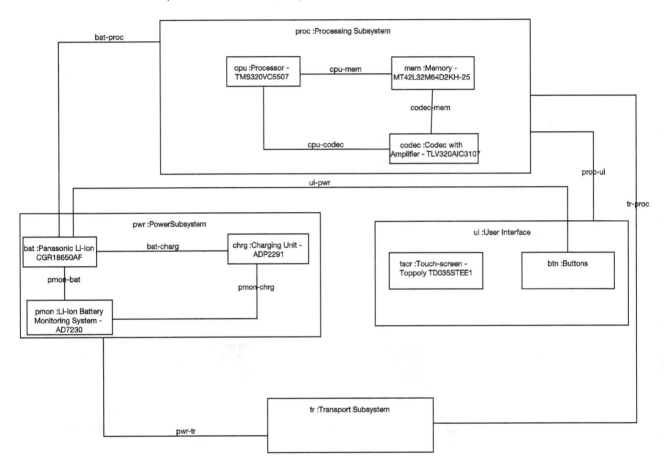

Figure 4-7. Audio Player Processing Subsytem Block Internals

Define Ports

The final step in our Roadmap for Modeling Structure is to define the Ports. Figure 4-8 illustrates data flow between the User Interface, Processing Subsystem, Transport Subsystem, and the USB and RS-232 connectors on the Audio Player.

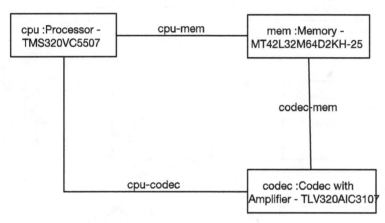

Figure 4-8. Audio Player Dataflow between Subsystems

Figure 4-8 illustrates a type of Port called a flowPort. The SysML flowPort is typed by a FlowSpecification which describes the properties and behavior associated with the port.

A flowPort describes also the directionality of the items flowing through it (in/out/conjugate) SysML also includes standardPorts, which can either provide an interface or require an interface. ItemFlows on the connectors (the arrows) describes what is flowing across the connections and through the ports. In the example above, it is Data which flows through these connections.

Audio Player Hardware Components

Finally, Figure 4-9 shows the hardware components of our Audio Player.

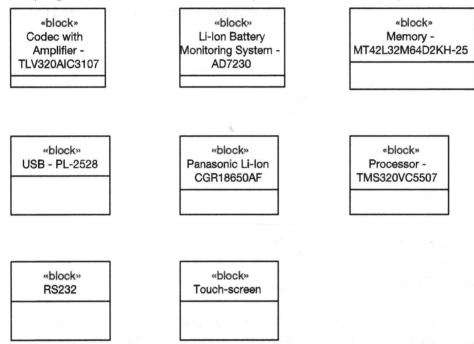

Figure 4-9. Hardware Components are modeled as Blocks

Modeling the hardware components as blocks makes it possible to allocate requirements to hardware. Enterprise Architect makes it easy to allocate requirements to any of the model elements discussed in this chapter.

This concludes our discussion of Blocks, Parts, and Ports. We've built the foundation for our SysML model over the previous 3 chapters where we covered Requirements, Behavior Modeling, and Structural Modeling. The final 3 chapters in the SysML section of the book introduce more advanced aspects of SysML and powerful capabilities of Enterprise Architect System Engineering Edition. In the next chapter we'll introduce Constraints and Parametrics, and then proceed to hardware and software implementation.

CHAPTER 5

Audio Player Constraints and Parametrics

One of the biggest differences between SysML and UML is the ability to simulate portions of a SysML model, based on mathematical and physical laws that describe key aspects of the system. One of the biggest differences between Enterprise Architect Systems Engineering Edition and other SysML modeling tools is Enterprise Architect's ability to do that simulation within the modeling tool, as opposed to simply interfacing to external simulators. We'll explore these capabilities in this chapter, starting, as usual, with our process roadmap.

Constraints and Parametrics Roadmap

Our constraints and parametrics roadmap has two sections. The first step, detailed in Figure 5-1, is to define the Constraints and Parametrics. The second step, shown in Figure 5-2, is to configure and run the Simulation. This entire process can be done completely within the Enterprise Architect Systems Engineering Edition—speeding convergence towards an engineering solution that meets the Requirements. We'll spend the remainder of this chapter following the steps in our roadmap for the Audio Player.

Start defining constraints and parametrics

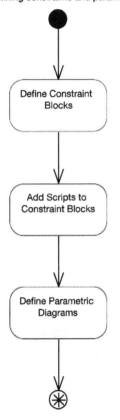

Simulate Parametric Models

Figure 5-1. Roadmap: Define Constraints and Parametrics

SysML parametric models support the engineering analysis of critical system parameters, including the evaluation of key metrics such as performance, reliability and other physical characteristics. They unite requirements models with system design models by capturing executable constraints based on complex mathematical relationships. In SysML, parametric models can also be used to describe the requirements themselves (e.g. "The internal combustion engine shall deliver its torque in accordance with the 'attached' parametric characteristics." The parametric can describe the graph used to describe the torque curve for the engine).

As you can see in Figure 5-1, defining parametric models using Enterprise Architect's System Engineering Edition involves defining Constraint Blocks, Adding Scripts to the Constraint Blocks, and Defining Parametric Diagrams.

Once the parametric models are defined, they can be simulated, as shown in Figure 5-2.

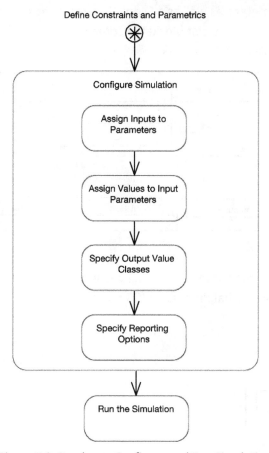

Figure 5-2. Roadmap: Configure and Run Simulation

Simulating a SysML parametric model is simply a matter of configuring the simulation, and then running it. Having the ability to do all of this within Enterprise Architect makes it much faster and easier to make engineering tradeoffs in the model without having to break away from Enterprise Architect into another tool, and tightens the engineering feedback loop, making it much faster to converge on a solution that meets your project's Requirements.

Define Constraint Blocks

To build a parametric model, you create a collection of SysML Constraint Blocks that formally describe the function of a constraint in a simulation model. Each Constraint Block contains properties that describe its input and output parameters, as well as a Script that describes the constraint's executable component. Figure 5-3 shows constraint blocks for some of the underlying mathematical functions that make our Audio Player work.

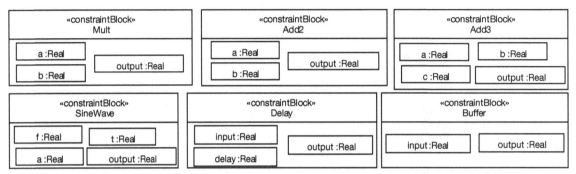

Figure 5-3. Constraint Blocks for Audio Player functions

Next, create a SysML Constraint Block to contain the Parametric model you wish to simulate. In Figure 5-4 we're going to simulate the Echo Digital Signal Processing (DSP) function.

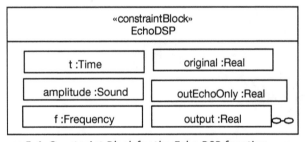

Figure 5-4. Constraint Block for the Echo DSP function

As you can see in Figure 5-4, our Echo function takes an original signal which is a sine wave amplitude and frequency, and delays that signal by some amount of time to produce an echo, then can output either the echo signal only, or a composite signal that adds the echo to the original signal. To do this, We'll make use of the "primitive" constraint blocks shown in Figure 5-3 for Sinewave, Delay, Add, etc.

Add Scripts to Constraint Blocks

Once your constraint blocks have been created, It's time to add Scripts. This is where you express the relationship / behavior of the constraint block as an executable script. In Enterprise

Architect, right-click on each of the Constraint Blocks and select the SysML | Add Element Script context menu option to add a script to the constraint block.

Figure 5-5 shows a script for the SineWave constraint block. Similar scripts exist for the Buffer, Delay, Add, and other constraint blocks.

```
1   var w = f*2*Maths.PI;
2   output = a * Maths.sin(w*t);
```

Figure 5-5. Script for the SineWave Constraint Block

Attaching scripts to constraint blocks provides the underlying mathematical foundation for running simulations. The precise behavior of each block is specified in equation form, using the inputs and outputs by name where appropriate, thus allowing the simulation to take place.

Modeling Tip: Enterprise Architect supports scripting in several languages

Scripts can be written in either JavaScript, Jscript or VBScript, and the user can use any other assemblies, components, or APIs in their constraint block script.

Note that simulating a constraint block requires the script across all constraint blocks to be written in the same language.

Define Parametric Diagrams

The Parametric model contains properties and occurrences of constraint blocks as Constraint Property elements, connected in a Parametric Diagram (see Figure 5-6).

The parametric diagram connects instances of primitive constraint blocks together to transform a set of inputs into a set of outputs. In Figure 5-6, we're taking an input SineWave, delaying and attenuating it, then adding that signal to the original input SineWave to produce an Echo effect. You can adjust parameters like attenuation and offset, and simulate, until you've produced the desired effect.

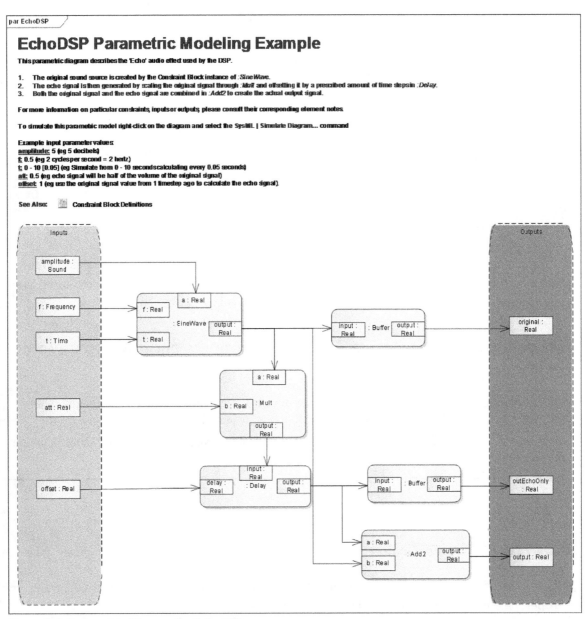

Figure 5-6. Parametric Diagram for Echo DSP

This brings us to the second portion of our roadmap, Configuring and Executing the Simulation.

Configure Simulation

Now that your constraint blocks, scripts, and parametrics have been defined, you're ready to simulate, so let's right-click within a Parametric Diagram and select the SysML | Simulate Diagram... context menu option. The Simulation Configuration dialog displays (see Figure 5-7).

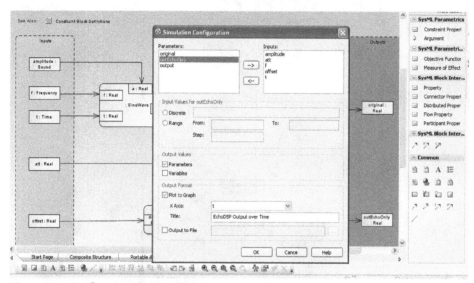

Figure 5-7. Configuring the Simulation

Fill out the Simulation Configuration dialog as follows:

- Assign Inputs. The Parameters panel lists all of the parameters that can be assigned input. Select each of the required parameters and click on the right arrow button to assign them as input. Parameters designated as input parameters are listed in the Inputs panel on the right. There must be at least one input parameter assigned for the simulation to execute.
- Assign a set of values for each of the designated input parameters. For each input parameter, in the Input Values panel select one of the two possible value kinds: Discrete or Range.
- Specify the classes of output value: Parameters or Variables.
- Specify how the simulation results are to be reported. The Output Format panel enables you to choose how the simulation outputs the simulation data. Depending on your configuration selections, the simulation's results are either written to a comma-separated CSV file or graphed in a 2-dimensional plot.

Once you've completed configuring your simulation, you're just about done.

Run the Simulation

To simulate your SysML model, click on the OK button to execute (Figure 5-8 shows the simulation results).

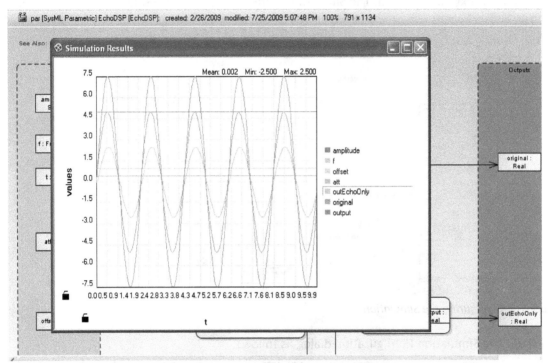

Figure 5-8. Simulation results can be displayed directly within Enterprise Architect.

While there is an option to export the simulation results to a CSV file, the ability to display simulation results directly within Enterprise Architect is one of the features that sets it apart from other SysML modeling tools. Having everything in a single tool makes it quick and easy to tweak design parameters so that your system meets its required performance targets.

In the next two chapters, we'll explore how Enterprise Architect helps to transform a SysML model into both hardware and software solutions.

CHAPTER 6

Audio Player Hardware Implementation

We discussed Behavioral Modeling with State Machines in Chapter 3. In this chapter, we'll demonstrate how to generate Hardware Description Language (HDL) code for State Machines, using our Audio Player Example. Then in Chapter 7 we'll explore software implementation.

Hardware Implementation Roadmap

Our Roadmap for implementing hardware via generating HDL code provides three parallel paths: implementation via VHDL, Verilog, and System-C. In all three cases, You'll leverage Enterprise Architect's unique ability to generate code from State Machines, and its powerful code-generation template capability.

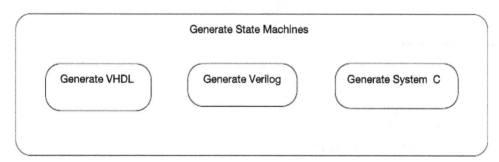

Figure 6-1. Hardware Implementation Roadmap with support for three popular Hardware Description Langauges

Audio Player Hardware Implementation

As usual, we'll illustrate our Roadmap using the Audio Player example. In this case, We'll explore the "Playback" operation and illustrate its implementation in VHDL, Verilog, and System C.

Figure 2 shows the top level package organization of the "Implementation" part of our Audio Player Model. We'll explore the software package in the next chapter. For the remainder of this chapter, we'll discuss code generation for State Machines, and present three flavors of generated HDL code for Playback.

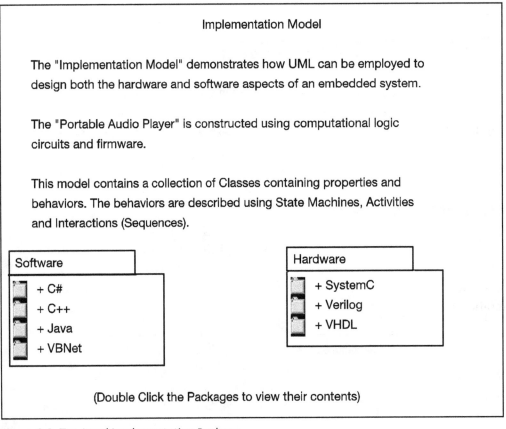

Figure 6-2. Top Level Implementation Package

Let's explore the Hardware package in more detail.

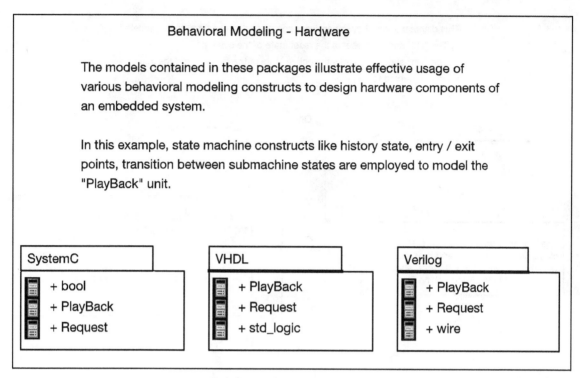

Figure 6-3. Enterprise Architect can generate HDL code for several languages.

As you'll see, all three of our State Machine implementations use a common design pattern. In each case, the Playback class contains a state machine with On and Off states. The On state contains a child diagram (sub-state-machine) that contains the actual design.

There are three steps in building an HDL State Machine model:

1. Designate Driving Triggers
2. Establish Port–Trigger Mapping
3. Define Active State Logic

Let's look at each of these in turn.

1. Designate Driving Triggers

The top level State Machine diagram should be used to model the different modes of a hardware component, and the associated triggers that drive them, as shown in Figure 6-4.

This diagram shows how a hardware component is expected to be modeled.
1. The "Off" state represents the reset state of the system
2. The "On" state represents the active state of the system, and the actual logic is expected to be here

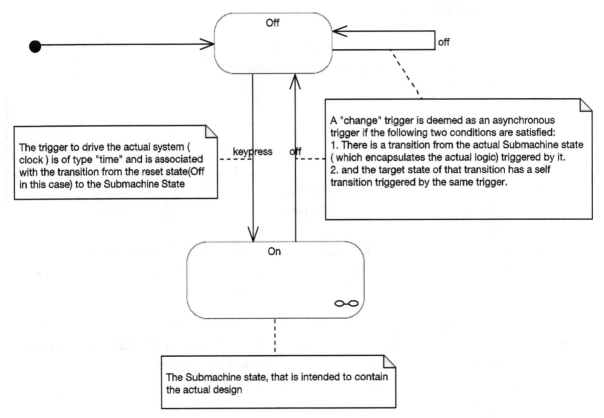

Figure 6-4. The top level state machine is used to designate operating modes and driving triggers.

There are several types of triggers.

Asynchronous Triggers

Asynchronous triggers should be modeled according to the following pattern:

- The trigger should be of type Change (specification: true / false).
- The active state (Submachine State) should have a transition trigger by it.
- The target state of the triggered transition should have a self transition with the same trigger.

Clock

A trigger of type time, which triggers the transitions to the active state (Submachine State) is deemed as the Clock. The specification of this trigger should be specific to the target language.

Table 6-1. Clock Trigger Specifications

Trigger Type	Language	Specification	
		Positive Edge Triggered	Negative Edge Triggered
Time	VHDL	rising_edge	falling_edge
	Verilog	posedge	negedge
	SystemC	positive	negative

2. Establish Port–Trigger Mapping

After successfully modeling the different operating modes of the component, and the triggers associated with them, you must associate the triggers with the component's ports as shown in Figure 6-5.

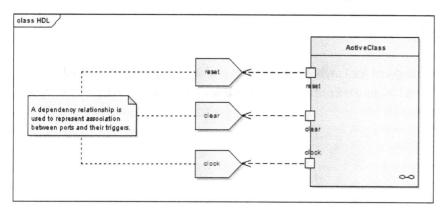

Figure 6-5. Dependency relationships are used to map ports to triggers

3. Define Active State Logic

The first two aspects, above, put in place the preliminaries required for efficient interpretation of the hardware components. The actual State Machine logic is now modeled within the Active (Submachine) state—see Figure 6-6.

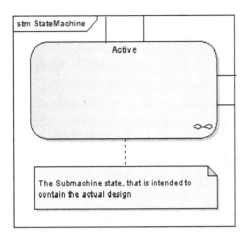

Figure 6-6. Active logic is specified on the child submachine for the Active state

We'll explore Step 3 in some detail for VHDL, Verilog, and System C.

Implementation in VHDL

Figure 6-7 shows a class diagram for Playback, with input and output ports designated. The design of the Playback functionality is contained in a multi-level state machine that's nested within the PlayBack class.

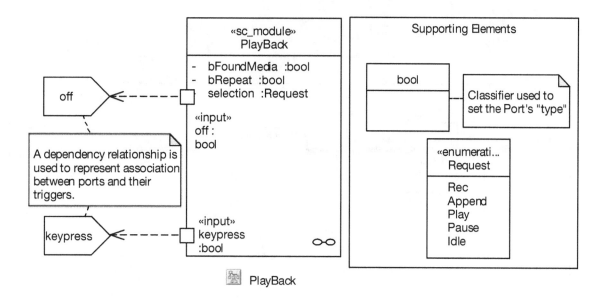

Figure 6-7. VHDL code will be generated from substates nested within the Playback class

The State Machine shown in Figure 6-8 is essentially the same for the Verilog and System C implementations. The differences are so minor that we won't repeat the diagram in the upcoming sections on those HDLs.

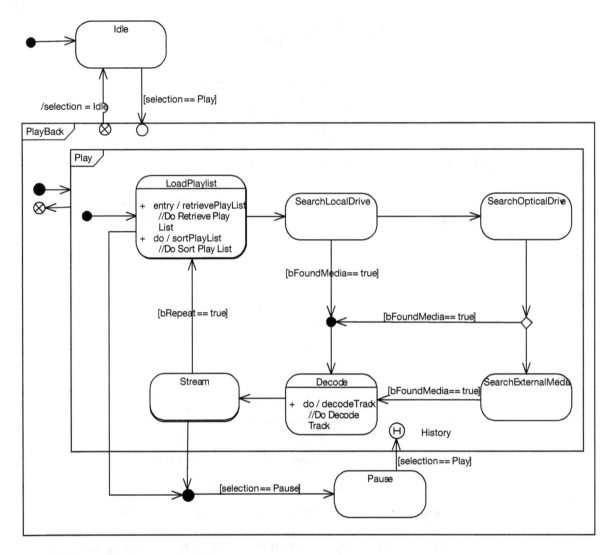

Figure 6-8. State Machine for Playback

VHDL Code Generation and Reverse Engineering

An Overview of VHDL

Here's a brief summary of VHDL that we extracted from Wikipedia.[41]

VHDL (VHSIC (Very High Speed Integrated Circuits) hardware description language) is commonly used as a design-entry language for field-programmable gate arrays and application-specific integrated circuits in electronic design automation of digital circuits.

VHDL was originally developed at the behest of the US Department of Defense in order to document the behavior of the ASICs that supplier companies were including in equipment. That is to say, VHDL was developed as an alternative to huge, complex manuals which were subject to implementation-specific details.

The idea of being able to simulate this documentation was so obviously attractive that logic simulators were developed that could read the VHDL files. The next step was the development of logic synthesis tools that read the VHDL, and output a definition of the physical implementation of the circuit. Modern synthesis tools can extract RAM, counter, and arithmetic blocks out of the code, and implement them according to what the user specifies. Thus, the same VHDL code could be synthesized differently for lowest area, lowest power consumption, highest clock speed, or other requirements.

VHDL is a fairly general-purpose language, and it doesn't require a simulator on which to run the code. There are many VHDL compilers, which build executable binaries. It can read and write files on the host computer, so a VHDL program can be written that generates another VHDL program to be incorporated in the design being developed. Because of this general-purpose nature, it is possible to use VHDL to write a testbench that verifies the functionality of the design using files on the host computer to define stimuli, interacts with the user, and compares results with those expected.

The key advantage of VHDL when used for systems design is that it allows the behavior of the required system to be described (modeled) and verified (simulated) before synthesis tools translate the design into real hardware (gates and wires).
Another benefit is that VHDL allows the description of a concurrent system (many parts, each with its own sub-behavior, working together at the same time). VHDL is a Dataflow language, unlike procedural computing languages such as BASIC, C, and assembly code, which all run sequentially, one instruction at a time.

A final point is that when a VHDL model is translated into the "gates and wires" that are mapped onto a programmable logic device such as a CPLD or FPGA, then it is the actual hardware being configured, rather than the VHDL code being "executed" as if on some form of a processor chip.

---

[41] http://en.wikipedia.org/wiki/VHDL

Enterprise Architect supports round-trip engineering of VHDL, using the Stereotypes and Tagged Values shown in Tables 6-2 and 6-3.

Table 6-2. VHDL Stereotypes used by Enterprise Architect

Stereotype	Applies To	Corresponds To
architecture	Class	An architecture
asynchronous	Method	An asynchronous process
configuration	Method	A configuration
enumeration	Inner Class	An *enum* type
entity	Interface	An entity
part	Attribute	A component instantiation
port	Attribute	A port
signal	Attribute	A signal declaration
struct	Inner Class	A record definition
synchronous	Method	A synchronous process
typedef	Inner Class	A *type* or *subtype* definition

Table 6-3. VHDL Tagged Values used by Enterprise Architect

Tag	Applies To	Corresponds To
isGeneric	Attribute (port)	The port declaration in a generic interface
isSubType	Inner Class (typedef)	A subtype definition
kind	Attribute (signal)	The signal kind (e.g. *register*, *bus*)
mode	Attribute (port)	The port mode (*in*, *out*, *inout*, *buffer, linkage*)
por Figure 14—Playback class diagram for Verilog implementation tmap	Attribute (part)	The generic / port map of the component instantiated
sensitivity	Method (synchronous)	The sensitivity list of a synchronous process
type	Inner Class (typedef)	The type indication of a type declaration
typeNameSpace	Attribute (part)	The type namespace of the instantiated component

Figures 6-9 and 6-10 show a portion of the generated code produced by Enterprise Architect. The VHDL code generated is extremely detailed and robust.

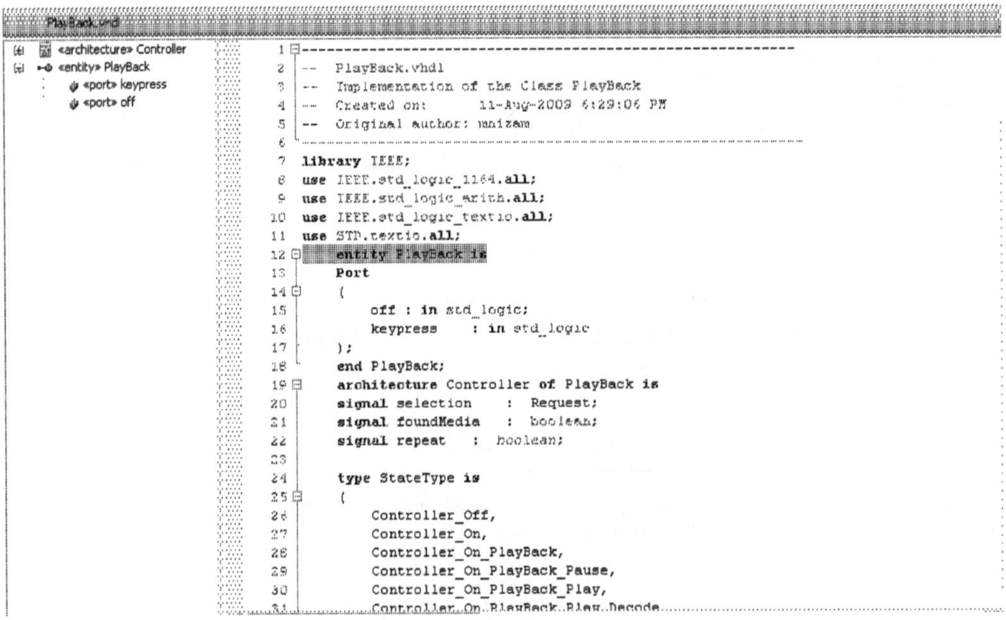

Figure 6-9. Enterprise Architect generates VHDL code from a state machine

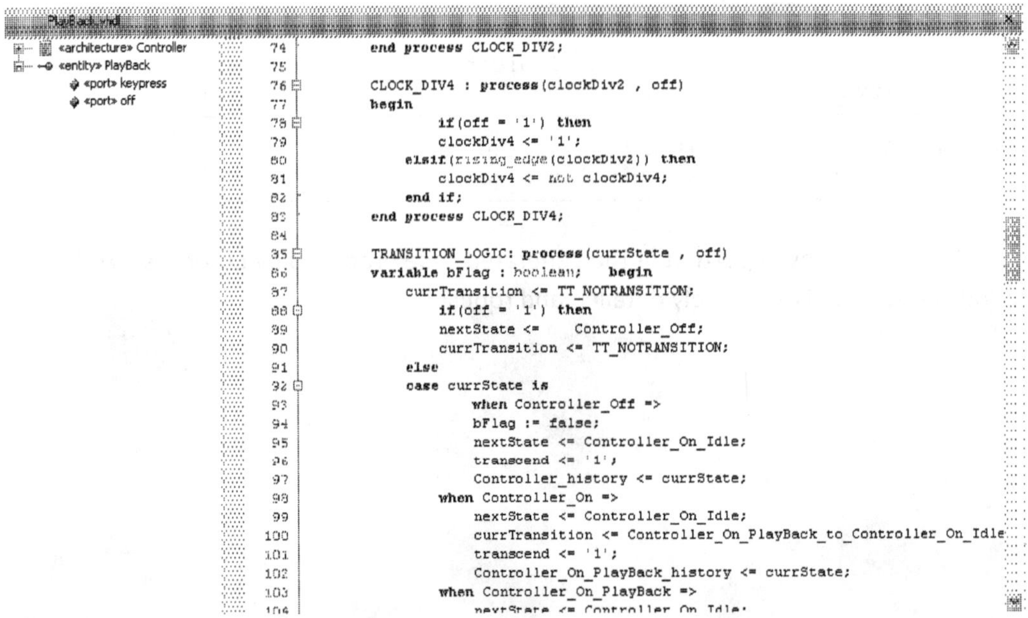

Figure 6-10. EA's state-machine code generator, combined with SysML parts and ports, and VHDL stereotypes and tagged values, produces a very complete implementation

Implementation in Verilog

Enterprise Architect supports round-trip engineering of Verilog[42] code, using the Stereotypes and Tagged Values shown in Tables 6-4 and 6-5.

Table 6-4. Verilog Stereotypes used by Enterprise Architect

Stereotype	Applies To	Corresponds To
asynchronous	Method	A concurrent process
enumeration	Inner Class	An enum type
initializer	Method	An initializer process
Module	Class	A module
Part	Attribute	A component instantiation
Port	Attribute	A port
synchronous	Method	A sequential process

Table 6-5. Verilog Tagged Values used by Enterprise Architect

Stereotype	Applies To	Corresponds To
Kind	Attribute (signal)	The signal kind (such as register, bus)
Mode	Attribute (port)	The port mode (in, out, inout)
Portmap	Attribute (part)	The generic/port map of the component instantiated
Sensitivity	Method	The sensitivity list of a sequential process
type	Attribute	The range or type value of an attribute

---

[42] See: http://en.wikipedia.org/wiki/Verilog

Implementation in SystemC

Enterprise Architect supports round-trip engineering of SystemC[43] code, using the following Stereotypes (Table 6-6) and Tagged Values (Table 6-7).

Table 6-6. System C stereotypes used by Enterprise Architect

Stereotype	Applies To	Corresponds To
delegate	Method	A delegate
enumeration	InnerClass	An enum type
friend	Method	A friend method
property	Method	A property definition
sc_ctor	Method	A SystemC constructor
sc_module	Class	A SystemC module
sc_port	Attribute	A port
sc_signal	Attribute	A signal
struct	InnerClass	A struct or union

Table 6-7. System C tagged values used by Enterprise Architect

Stereotype	Applies To	Corresponds To
Kind	Attribute (Port)	Port kind (clocked, fifo, master, slave, resolved, vector)
Mode	Attribute (Port)	Port mode (in, out, inout)
overrides	Method	The Inheritance list of a method declaration
throw	Method	The exception specification of a method

---

[43] See: http://en.wikipedia.org/wiki/System_C and www.systemc.org/home

CHAPTER 7

Audio Player Software Implementation

Enterprise Architect contains numerous features to help with code generation and reverse engineering, and also integrates closely with the Visual Studio and Eclipse development environments via its MDG Integration technology. Many of Enterprise Architect's code engineering capabilities, including forward and reverse engineering, and Enterprise Architect's powerful code template framework, are described in detail in the *Enterprise Architect for Power Users multimedia tutorial*.[44] This chapter will focus in on Sparx Systems' unique capability for Behavioral Code Generation, and on the MDG Integration capability.

Figure 7-1 shows our Roadmap for Software Implementation.

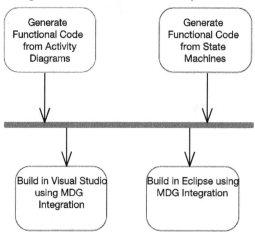

Figure 7-1. Roadmap for Software Implementation

---

[44] *Enterprise Architect for Power Users multimedia tutorial*: www.iconixsw.com/EA/PowerUsers.html

Modeling Tip: Behavioral Models can be code generated

Enterprise Architect enables you to define an element's behavior through the element's operations and parameters. You can also define the behavior of more specific behavioral elements such as Activities, Interactions, Actions and Interaction Occurrences.

In this chapter, we'll explore how to transform behavior models of the type that you saw in Chapter 3 into executable source code in C#, C++, Java, and Visual Basic. Figure 7-2 shows the top level package diagram from our audio player example, which we'll use to illustrate behavioral code generation.

Behavioral Modeling - Software

Models in this package illustrates usage of various commonly used behavioral constructs.

States' behaviors to invoke another behavior, Activity diagram constructs like call actions, patterns to model control statements, loops and Sequence diagram constructs like synchronous messages, return messages, combined fragments, etc are employed to create the model.

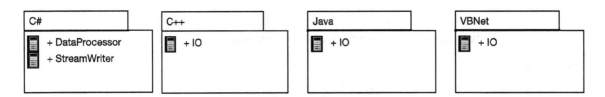

Figure 7-2. Audio Player example organization for behavioral code generation

In addition to its long-standing ability to generate code for software classes, Enterprise Architect supports generation of code from three UML behavioral modeling paradigms:

- State Machine diagrams
- Interaction diagrams
- Activity diagrams

We'll explore behavioral code generation in considerable detail in this chapter, and it should be an interesting ride to some places you've probably never been to before, so fasten your seat belts. We'll start off with a look at generating C# code from state machines and activity diagrams, for the DataProcessor class from our audio player.

Data Processor: C# code gen from State and Activity Diagrams

Figure 7-3 shows a class diagram for the `DataProcessor` class, which contains a nested state machine for `Searching External Media`, and a nested Activity Diagram for `Appending to a Buffer`. Figure 7-4 shows the nesting of behaviors on a Composite Structure Diagram.

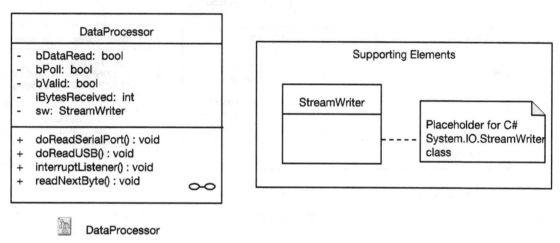

The DataProcessor class reads data
from external inputs, and processes it.

DataProcessor

The State machine in this example illustrates modeling transitions to history
states, entry / exit points, transitions between SubMachineStates, etc.

The Activity diagrams shows modeling multithreaded applications using
fork / join, invoking other behaviors using Call actions, etc.

Figure 7-3. DataProcessor Class Diagram

For more information on Code Generation from State Machine Diagrams refer to:

Code Generation - State Machine Diagrams

For more information on Code Generation from Activity Diagrams refer to:

Code Generation - Activity Diagrams

For more information on Code Generation from Sequence Diagrams refer to:

Code Generation - Sequence Diagrams

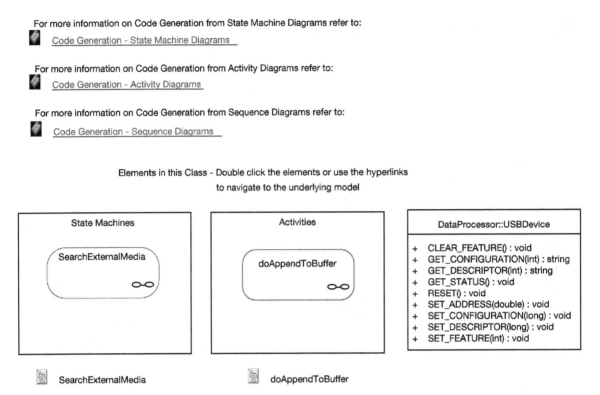

Elements in this Class - Double click the elements or use the hyperlinks
to navigate to the underlying model

Figure 7-4. Composite Structure Diagram illustrating the nested behaviors of DataProcessor

Behavioral code generation in Enterprise Architect requires the behavioral diagrams to be nested within the "Active Class" (the class that gets generated). Figure 7-5 shows the organization in Enterprise Architect's project browser.

Figure 7-5. Behaviors to be code generated are nested within a parent class

Behavioral Code Generation from State Machines

A State Machine that's nested within a Class generates the following constructs to enable effective execution of the States" do, entry and exit behaviors and also to code the appropriate transition's effect when necessary.

Enumerations

StateType—comprises an enumeration for each of the States contained within the State Machine

TransitionType—comprises an enumeration for each transition that has a valid effect associated with it, e.g. ProcessOrder_Delivered_to_ProcessOrder_Closed

CommandType—comprises an enumeration for each of the behavior types that a State can contain (Do, Entry, Exit).

Attributes

currState:StateType—a variable to hold the current State's information

nextState:StateType—a variable to hold the next State's information, set by each State's transitions accordingly

currTransition:TransitionType—a variable to hold the current transition information; this is set if the transition has a valid effect associated with it

transcend:Boolean—a flag used to advise if a transition is involved in transcending between different State Machines (or Submachine states)

xx_history:StateType—a history variable for each State Machine/Submachine State, to hold information about the last State from which the transition took place.

Operations

StatesProc—a States procedure, containing a map between a State's enumeration and its operation; it de-references the current State's information to invoke the respective State's function

TransitionsProc—a Transitions procedure, containing a map between the Transition's enumeration and its effect; it invokes the respective effect

<<State>>—an operation for each of the States contained within the State Machine; this renders a State's behaviors based on the input CommandType, and also executes its transitions

initializeStateMachine—a function that initializes all the framework-related attributes

runStateMachine—a function that iterates through each State, and executes their behaviors and transitions accordingly.

Figure 7-6 shows the state machine for `SearchExternalMedia`, and you can see a bit of the automatically generated code for the Do, Entry, and Exit states in Figure 7-7. The complete behavior of the state machine is generated automatically.

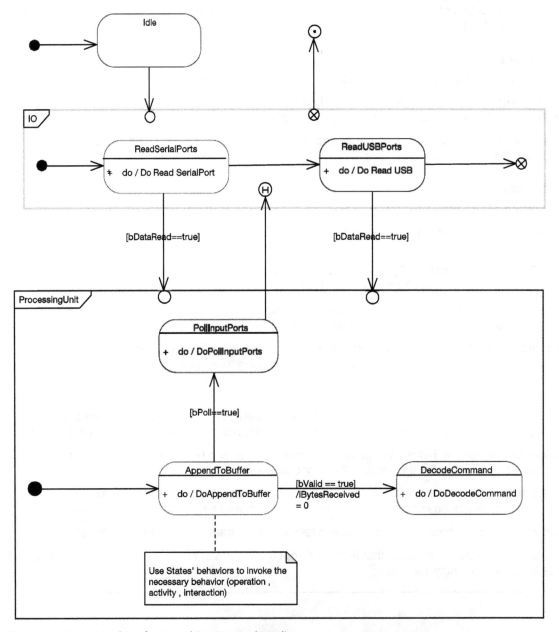

Figure 7-6. State Machine for Searching External Media

The `ProcessingUnit` Polls its Input Ports, Appends to a Buffer, and Decodes Commands. We'll see the nested activity diagram and generated code for `AppendToBuffer` in Figures 7-8 and 7-9. But first, Figure7-7 shows generated code for the state machine shown in Figure 7-6.

```
DataProcessor.cs

155
156        /* Begin - EA generated code for StateMachine */
157
158
159        private enum StateType : int
160        {
161               SearchExternalMedia,
162            SearchExternalMedia_ProcessingUnit,
163            SearchExternalMedia_ProcessingUnit_PollInputPorts,
164            SearchExternalMedia_ProcessingUnit_AppendToBuffer,
165            SearchExternalMedia_ProcessingUnit_DecodeCommand,
166            SearchExternalMedia_IO,
167            SearchExternalMedia_IO_ReadUSBPorts,
168            SearchExternalMedia_IO_ReadSerialPorts,
169            SearchExternalMedia_Idle,
170            ST_NOSTATE
171        }
172        private enum TransitionType : int
173        {
174               SearchExternalMedia_ProcessingUnit_AppendToBuffer_to_SearchExternalM
175            TT_NOTRANSITION
176        }
177        private enum CommandType : int
178        {
179            Do,
180            Entry,
181            Exit
182        }
183        private StateType currState;
```

Figure 7-7. Enterprise Architect generates Behavioral Code for State Machines

Behavioral Code Generation from Activity Diagrams

Enterprise Architect uses a system engineering graph optimizer to analyze an activity diagram and render it into various code-generatable constructs. The constructs are also transformed into one of the various action types (if appropriate), similar to Interaction diagram constructs.

Conditional Statements

To model a conditional statement, you use Decision/Merge nodes. Alternatively, you can imply Decisions/Merges internally. The graph optimizer expects an associated Merge node for each Decision node, to facilitate efficient tracking of various branches and analysis of the code constructs within them.

Invocation Actions (Call Operation Action, Call Behavior Action)

Call Actions are handled more efficiently. Each action has arguments relating to the parameters of the associated behavior (use the Synchronize button of the Arguments dialog to synchronize arguments and parameters).

Atomic Actions

Atomic actions contain implementation-specific statements that are rendered "in line" as a sequence of code statements in a procedure.

Loops

Enterprise Architect's system engineering graph optimizer is also capable of analyzing and identifying loops. An identified loop is internally rendered as an Action Loop, which is translated by the EASL code generation macros to generate the required code.

Figure 7-8 shows an activity diagram for `AppendToBuffer`, and Figure 7- 9 shows a snip of the resulting C# code.

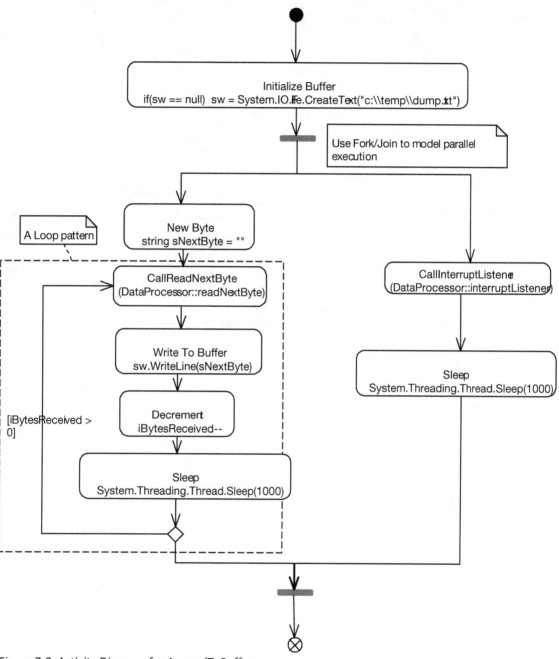

Figure 7-8. Activity Diagram for AppendToBuffer

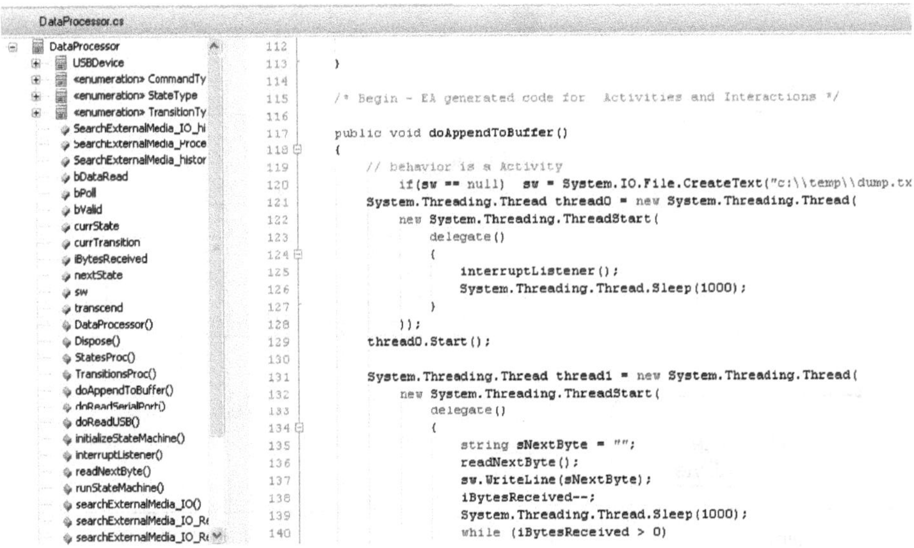

```
DataProcessor.cs
DataProcessor                          112
  USBDevice                            113        }
  <enumeration> CommandTy              114
  <enumeration> StateType              115        /* Begin - EA generated code for  Activities and Interactions */
  <enumeration> TransitionTy           116
  SearchExternalMedia_IO_hi            117    public void doAppendToBuffer()
  SearchExternalMedia_Proce            118    {
  SearchExternalMedia_histor           119        // behavior is a Activity
  bDataRead                            120            if(sw == null)  sw = System.IO.File.CreateText("c:\\temp\\dump.tx
  bPoll                                121        System.Threading.Thread thread0 = new System.Threading.Thread(
  bValid                               122            new System.Threading.ThreadStart(
  currState                            123                delegate()
  currTransition                       124                {
  iBytesReceived                       125                    interruptListener();
  nextState                            126                    System.Threading.Thread.Sleep(1000);
  sw                                   127                }
  transcend                            128            ));
  DataProcessor()                      129        thread0.Start();
  Dispose()                            130
  StatesProc()                         131        System.Threading.Thread thread1 = new System.Threading.Thread(
  TransitionsProc()                    132            new System.Threading.ThreadStart(
  doAppendToBuffer()                   133                delegate()
  doReadSerialPort()                   134                {
  doReadUSB()                          135                    string sNextByte = "";
  initializeStateMachine()             136                    readNextByte();
  interruptListener()                  137                    sw.WriteLine(sNextByte);
  readNextByte()                       138                    iBytesReceived--;
  runStateMachine()                    139                    System.Threading.Thread.Sleep(1000);
  searchExternalMedia_IO()             140                    while (iBytesReceived > 0)
  searchExternalMedia_IO_R
  searchExternalMedia_IO_R
```

Figure 7-9. Generated C# code for AppendToBuffer

Once again, the *full detail of the behavior detailed on the diagram is automatically generated into code*.

IO Code generation in C++, Java, and VB.Net

In this section, we'll look inside the IO class and explore behavioral code generation in C++, Java, and VB.Net. Figure 7-10 shows the class diagram for the C++ branch of the model; similar diagrams (not shown here) appear in the Java and VB packages.

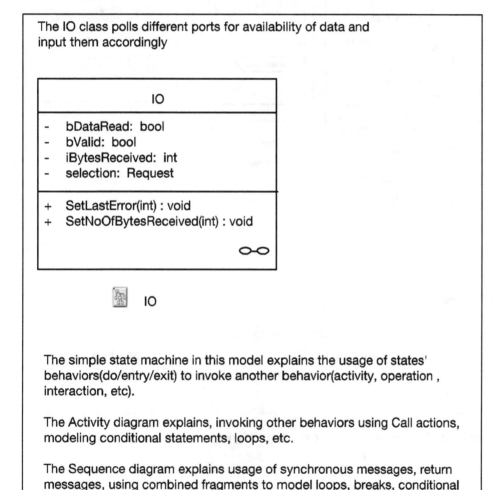

Figure 7-10. IO class diagram

As with the DataProcessor example, all behaviors which we'd like to code generate are nested within the IO class (see Figure 7-11).

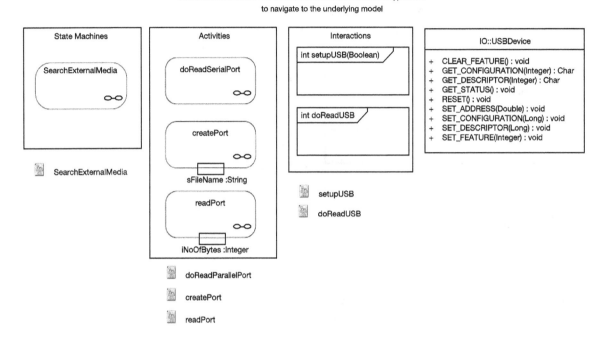

Figure 7-11. Nested Behaviors of IO

We'll explore code generation from Interaction, State, and Activity Diagrams. Figure 7-12 shows the sequence diagram for Setting up the USB port, and Figure 7-13 shows how to Read the USB port. Figure 7-14 shows a fragment of the automatically generated C++ code.

Code Generation from Sequence Diagrams

Code generation from sequence diagrams that are nested within a Class uses Enterprise Architect's system engineering graph optimizer to transform the diagram into code. **Messages** and **Fragments** are identified as one of the several action types based on their functionality, and the EASL code generation templates are used to render their behavior accordingly. For example:

A Message that invokes an operation is identified as *an Action Call* and is rendered accordingly

Combined Fragments are identified by their types and conditions; for instance, an *Alt* fragment is identified as an *Action If*, and a loop fragment is identified as an *Action Loop*.

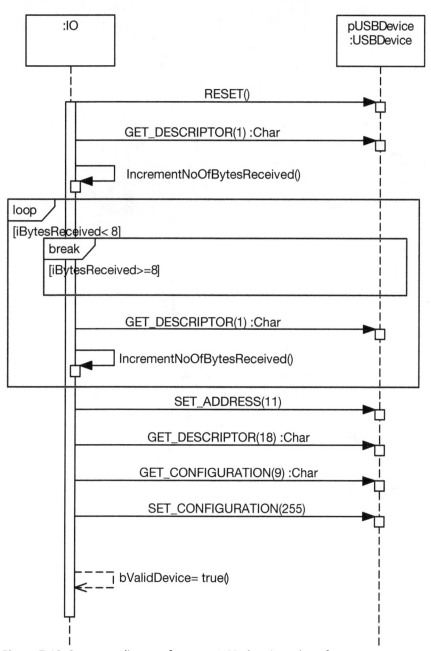

Figure 7-12. Sequence diagram for setup USB showing a loop fragment

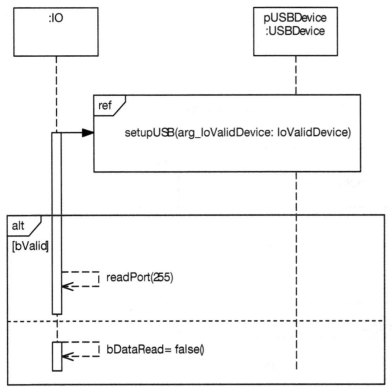

Figure 7-13. Reading the USB Port

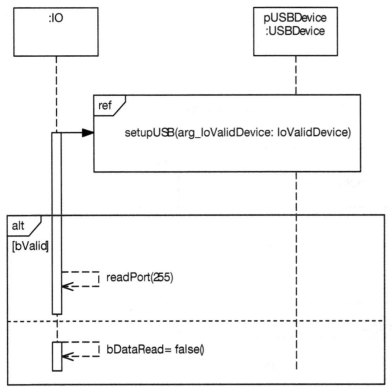

Figure 7-14. Generated C++ code for IO

Generating VB.Net and Java from State and Activity Diagrams

Hopefully by now you're getting the idea that Enterprise Architect can generate behavioral code in just about any language from state, activity, and sequence diagrams. We'll illustrate this first by showing VB.Net code (Figure 7-16) for the Search External Media state machine (Figure 7-15).

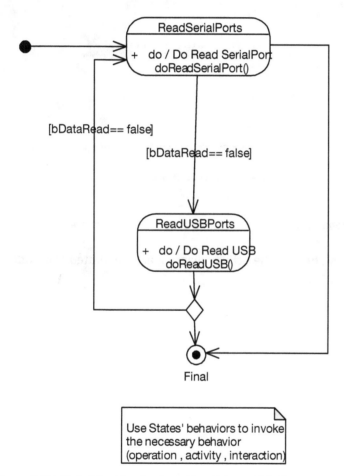

Figure 7-15. State Machine for Searching External Media

```
IO.vb
IO                          160
  USBDevice                 161          TT_NOTRANSITION
  «enumeration» CommandType 162    End Enum
  «enumeration» StateType   163    Private Enum CommandType
  «enumeration» TransitionType 164      BehDo
  SearchExternalMedia_history 165       BehEntry
  bDataRead                 166          BehExit
  bValid                    167    End Enum
  bValidPort                168    private currState As StateType
  currState                 169    private nextState As StateType
  currTransition            170    private currTransition As TransitionType
  iBytesReceived            171    private transcend as Boolean
  nextState                 172        private SearchExternalMedia_history As StateType
  transcend                 173    Private sub searchExternalMedia_ReadSerialPorts(ByVal comma
  IncrementNoOfBytesReceived( 174      Select Case command
  StatesProc(StateType, Commar 175        case CommandType.BehDo
  TransitionsProc(TransitionType) 176        'Do Behaviors..
  createPort(String)        177            doReadSerialPort()
  doReadSerialPort()        178            'State's Transitions
  doReadUSB()               179            Dim bFlag as Boolean
  initializeStateMachine()  180            If (bDataRead = false) Then
  readPort(Integer)         181                bFlag = true
  runStateMachine()         182                nextState = StateType.SearchExternalMedia_R
  searchExternalMedia_ReadSeri 183           End If
  searchExternalMedia_ReadJSB 184            If ( bFlag = False ) Then
  setupUSB(Boolean)         185                nextState = StateType.ST_NOSTATE'Final Stat
                            186            End If
                            187        End Select
                            188    End Sub
```

Figure 7-16. VB.Net behavioral code, automatically generated from the state machine above

Finally, we'll wrap up this section by showing the activity diagram and generated Java code for Read Serial Port in Figures 7-17 and 7-18.

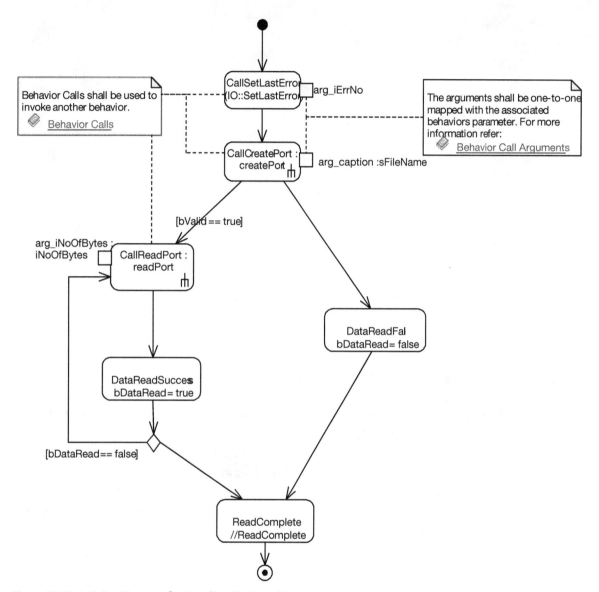

Figure 7-17. Activity Diagram for Reading the Serial Port

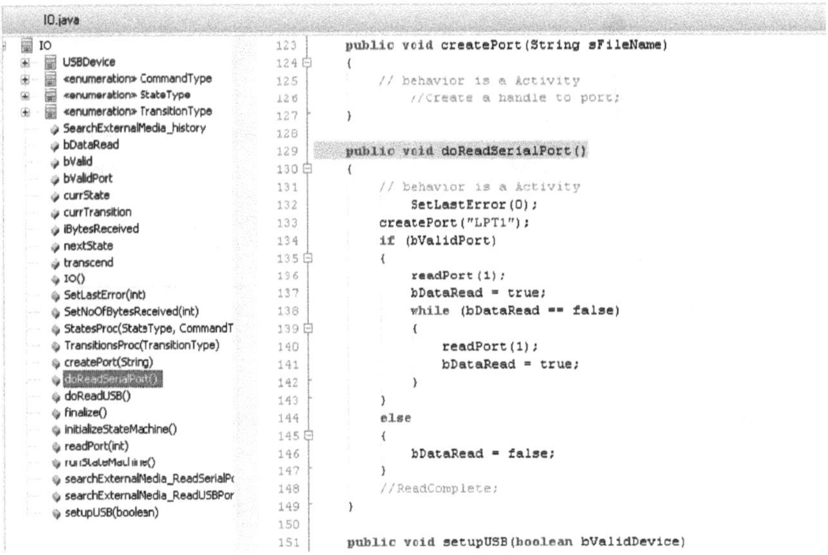

Figure 7-18. Behaviorally generated Java code for Read Serial Port

Customizing The Code Generator

Enterprise Architect uses a template-driven approach to code generation, and provides an editor for tailoring the code templates.

Enterprise Architect's code templates specify the transformation from UML elements to the various parts of a given programming language. The templates are written as plain text with a syntax that shares some aspects of both mark-up languages and scripting languages.

Figure 7-19 shows the Code Template Editor being used to tailor how C# code is generated.

Code Templates are written as plain text. The template syntax centers on three basic constructs:

- Literal Text
- Macros
- Variables

Templates can contain any or all of these constructs.

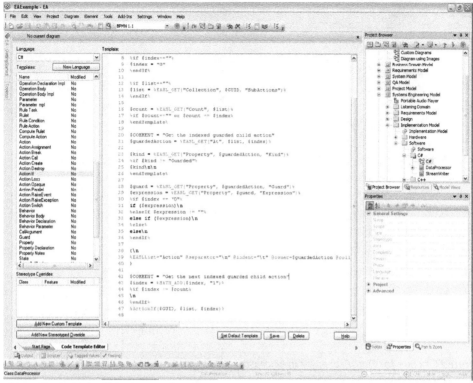

Figure 7-19. ActionIf Code template for C#

Integrating Models and Code in your favorite IDE

Since the beginning of modeling time, the gap (sometimes a chasm) between models and code has always been problematic. Models, the argument goes, don't represent reality... only the code represents reality... therefore the model must be worthless, and we should just skip modeling and jump straight to code.

Those who have used this argument to avoid modeling probably felt quite safe in doing so because nobody has ever managed to make "reverse engineering" or "round-trip engineering" a seamless process... until now. But that's exactly the problem that the MDG Integration technology (available for both Visual Studio and Eclipse) from Sparx solves.

So... here's the six million dollar question: how do we keep the model and the code synchronized over the lifetime of the project? You can see the answer in Figure 7-20.

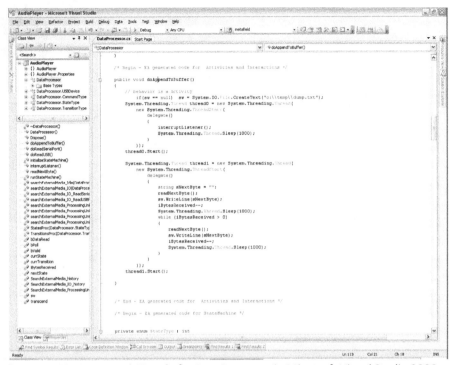

Figure 7-20. Generated C# code for DataProcessor in Microsoft Visual Studio 2008

Here's how it works:

1) Connect your UML model to a Visual Studio or Eclipse Project

2) Link a package in your model to the project in your IDE

3) Browse the source code by clicking on operations on the classes

4) Edit the source code in your IDE

MDG Integration keeps the model and code in-synch for you. Problem solved.

Wrapping up

That concludes our roadmap for embedded systems development using SysML and the Enterprise Architect System Engineering Edition. Our roadmap has taken us through Requirements definition, allocation, and traceability, hardware and software design, constraints and parametrics, and through implementation using behavioral code generation for software and for hardware using hardware-description languages.

We wish you success in your development efforts!

ROADMAP # 3

ICONIX PROCESS FOR SERVICE ORIENTED ARCHITECTURE

SOA Development—An Illustrated Example Using Enterprise Architect

by Doug Rosenberg

CHAPTER 1

A Roadmap for Service-Oriented Architecture Development using Enterprise Architect Business and Software Engineering Edition

Trying to make sense of the acronym soup that engulfs important topics like software architecture, business modeling, and service oriented architectures is a major challenge. We're going to take a shot at it in this book by following a single example all the way from architecture to code. The example is a Service-Oriented Architecture (SOA) car rental system that's implemented with a combination of web-services and custom software.

Along the way we'll illustrate many of the key features of *Enterprise Architect Business and Software Engineering Edition*. As with a number of other topics we've addressed in our books, we're going to use a Process Roadmap to tie everything together in what we hope will be a clear and understandable manner.

Why a Service-Oriented Architecture Example?

We didn't have to choose a Service-Oriented Architecture for our example project; SOA is one of many possible architectures that can be developed using EA's Business and Software Engineering Edition. But web services and SOA have become increasingly important in today's IT universe. A recent article from IBM Global Technology Services[45] suggests that nearly half the companies in the world are either adopting, piloting, or considering SOA, and that investments in these projects may reach between $18 Billion and $160 Billion in the near future. With those sorts of numbers, it stands to reason that many readers will be interested in a roadmap and a cohesive example that brings some clarity to the problem. Hopefully this includes you.

As it turns out, an SOA example also serves to illustrate many of the features of the Sparx Systems solution, which supports building "executable business processes" that use WSDL (Web Service Definition Language) to implement their solution. And, since projects don't live by web services alone, Enterprise Architect has numerous other useful features for handling those parts of the application that require custom (non-web service) development. In particular we'll spend a significant amount of time in this book exploring a new and unique capability for **behavioral code generation** for the enforcement of Business Rules, and tight integration with IDEs, including Eclipse and Visual Studio. We've leveraged the power of these capabilities into our SOA Roadmap.

The SOA Roadmap (aka "ICONIX Process for SOA Development")

As with all of the ICONIX Process Roadmaps[46], our SOA roadmap is defined as a set of activity diagrams. In this case, the roadmap provides a "cookbook" set of steps that can be followed for building systems that are based around an SOA.

Figure 1-1 shows our top-level roadmap. The chapter outline of this book follows this roadmap directly. Each of these top-level activities will expand out to a child diagram showing further detail. Those detailed activities will be discussed in the respective chapters—this chapter gives you the "big picture" overview.

---

[45] *Realizing Business Value from an Integrated Service-Oriented Architecture System in a Multivendor World* – IBM Global Technology Services, April 2008

[46] These now include roadmaps for Embedded Real-Time Systems, Testing (aka Design Driven Testing), Algorithm Intensive Development, and Business Modeling, in addition to ICONIX Process for Software (the original "Use Case Driven ICONIX Process"). See www.iconixsw.com for more details.

A Quick Introduction to SOA

Service-Oriented Architecture (SOA) is an approach to building complex software systems from a set of reusable services that obey service-orientation principles. Many people believe that SOAs can help businesses to be more "agile" -- in other words, enable faster and more cost-effective responses to changing conditions.

SOA enables construction of applications from fairly large chunks of reusable functionality that can be built quickly, primarily from existing services. Thus, SOA promotes reuse at a "macro" level, and, in theory, as an organization publishes more and more business functionality as services over time, the cost of building applications that use those services decreases.

A service that obeys the principles of service-orientation is an *autonomous, loosely coupled*, and *stateless* unit of functionality that is made available by a *formally defined interface*. The functionality provided by a service is *discoverable* by applications that use the service. In other words, services expose their functionality via interfaces that other applications and services can read to understand how to use them. Development of services can thus be decoupled from development of the applications that use them. The ***Universal Description Discovery and Integration*** (UDDI) specification defines a mechanism to publish and discover information about services.

Services are not allowed to call other services, but may communicate with them via messages. That is, services are loosely coupled, and each service implements a single action, such as placing an online rental car reservation. Services are also loosely coupled to underlying operating systems and insulate application code from specific technologies that are used to implement the services.

Services are designed without knowing who will be using them. In a service-oriented architecture, applications are built from services which communicate via messages using a process known as ***orchestration***.

A popular approach to implementing a service-oriented architecture is via web services, which make services accessible over the Internet independent of platforms and programming languages. The BPEL language is often used to orchestrate SOA applications. Building applications from services requires metadata that describes the characteristics of the services, and the data that is used. Typically, XML is used to describe data, WSDL describes the services themselves, and SOAP (Simple Object Access Protocol) describes communication between services.

Two important roles in developing service-oriented applications are that of the service provider and service requester. Service providers develop their services and publish them to a broker, while service requesters use the brokers to locate services, bind to them, and then use them.

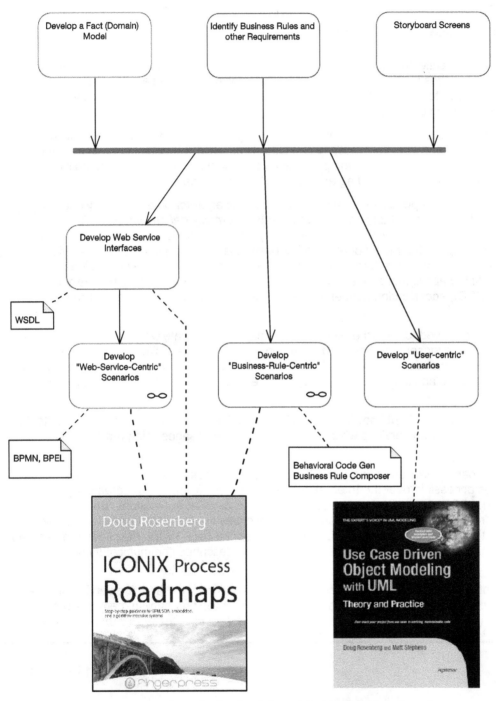

Figure 1-1. ICONIX Process Roadmap for Service-Oriented Architecture Development

As you can see, the top-level roadmap includes some "common stuff" like figuring out your requirements, and modeling the problem domain (we'll discuss the "common stuff" in Chapter 2), and then provides multiple paths for developing different flavors of business processes, all the way to code.

The roadmap diagram above reflects the philosophy that when you set out to implement a system using an SOA, there will effectively be a mix of 3 different kinds of scenarios:

1) **Scenarios that use web services** (for which we will develop web service interfaces using WSDL, and orchestrate the use of those web services using BPMN and BPEL.
2) **Scenarios that enforce business rules** (for which we will use activity diagrams and the business rule composer)
3) **Regular old software use cases** (which we won't discuss in this book because we've covered it quite thoroughly in my other books)

Most systems will contain a mix of these different types of scenarios.

In many cases (but not all), the *web service scenarios* will cross Business To Business (B2B) boundaries, e.g.: a car rental reservation system talking to a credit card company to run a payment transaction.

The *business rule scenarios* are more likely to be within the boundaries of one business, e.g. the car rental system enforcing eligibility rules on driver age, credit score, etc. There is little or no user interface in these business rule scenarios, so they can be completely code generated from an activity diagram using the business rule composer.

Finally there is the user interface. These would be the screens of the car rental system that the reservations agent accesses, and which would trigger the business rule checks and B2B transactions. These parts of the system are best modeled with use cases.

Where a business process can be implemented via web services, we follow the branch on the left: ***web service interface definition using WSDL, and orchestration using BPMN and BPEL***. We'll illustrate this with our Car Rental example in Chapters 2 and 3.

- For processes that are primarily focused on enforcing business rules, we take the right branch: ***Behavioral Code Generation from Activity Diagrams using the Business Rule Composer***. We'll explain how to use the business rule composer and talk about behavioral code generation in Chapter 4.
- And finally, for those user-centric processes that use a GUI, we model them following a *use case driven* approach that's out of scope for this book, but well documented in my

other books[47].

- With all of these branches, we can compile and build using either Eclipse or Visual Studio, and use the Sparx "MDG Integration" technology to keep models and code in-synch. We'll cover this capability in Chapter 5.

SOA, BPEL, WSDL—Publishing Your Services on the Web

In SOA-based systems, it's possible to implement many business processes by using previously developed "web services". The term "orchestration" is often used to describe implementing a business process by using a number of web services in a collaborative way. In order to better understand this concept, we need to begin explaining some acronyms. We'll give you a brief intro to web services in Chapter 2. For now, we'll start with these two definitions:

WSDL (Web Service Definition Language) is an XML-based language that describes web services and how to access them.

BPEL is actually short for Web Service Business Process Execution Language (WS-BPEL). BPEL defines business processes that interact with external entities that are defined using WSDL.

BPEL is an orchestration language that describes *messages to and from a business process*. Those messages are defined using WSDL.

Note that it's possible to draw BPMN (Business Process Modeling Notation) diagrams to model business processes without generating BPEL (Business Process Execution Language). And, you can model BPEL using other graphical notations besides BPMN. But one of the more interesting strategies, which we'll explore, involves *using BPMN to model BPEL processes*[48].

Figure 1-2 shows the roadmap basic steps for using BPMN to model BPEL, and generating WSDL.

---

[47] See *Use Case Driven Object Modeling with UML – Theory and Practice* by Doug Rosenberg and Matt Stephens, from Apress.

[48] We found *"Using BPMN to model a BPEL Process"* by Stephen A. White, IBM Corporation, to be a very useful article.

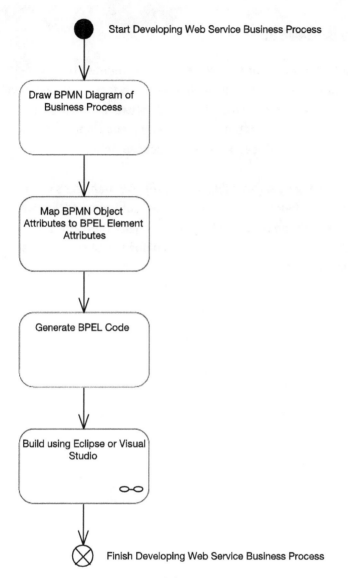

Figure 1-2. We use BPMN to model BPEL, then generate BPEL code

We'll develop web service interfaces using WSDL in Chapter 2, and then further illustrate our roadmap with a BPMN diagram and BPEL/WSDL code for our Car Rental System in Chapter 3.

Business Processes Must Satisfy Business Rules

Even in a service oriented system, not all business processes can be implemented by orchestrating web services. Some business processes will involve user interfaces, and some will be focused on enforcing business rules. We won't discuss GUI-based software use cases in this book, as that process is well documented elsewhere, but we will spend a fair amount of time discussing some new ways to implement those processes that are focused on enforcing business processes.

In Chapter 4 we'll introduce you to the unique capabilities of *Enterprise Architect*'s Business Rule Composer. Starting from the domain model (fact model) and the requirements that we'll present in Chapter 2, we'll take you through the process of creating Activity Diagrams for Business Processes, stereotyping Actions as RuleTasks, and finally, linking the business rules to the rule tasks in preparation for behavioral code generation.

Figure 1-3 shows how it works.

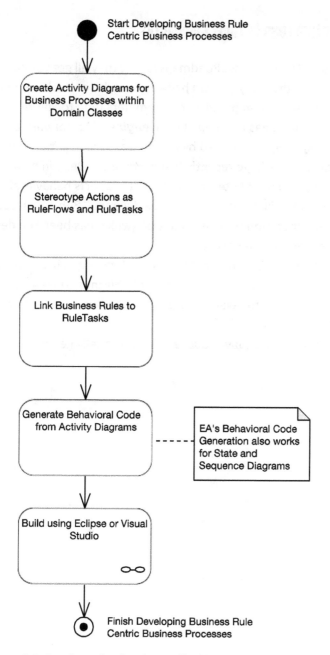

Figure 1-3. Roadmap for developing "business-rule-centric" scenarios using EA's Business Rule Composer

Once again, we'll illustrate our roadmap with an example of how to use the Rule Composer for our Car Rental System.

Behavioral Code Generation—A Quantum Leap in Tools Capability

One of the common themes of all of our ICONIX Process Roadmaps is that they all get you to code. We've always believed that processes that only get you halfway to code (or less) are much better in theory than they are in practice (because in practice, programmers tend to ignore them). Enterprise Architect, since its early days, has excelled at *code engineering* (forward and reverse engineering for a wide range of languages, powered by customizable code generation templates). But those already strong capabilities have recently taken a quantum leap in power.

The Business and Systems Engineering Edition of Enterprise Architect supports behavioral code generation from activity diagrams, state diagrams and sequence diagrams. Behavioral code generation is a major advancement over generation of "class headers" (which has been the de-facto meaning of "code generation" for more than a decade).

Enterprise Architect uniquely supports generation of complete algorithmic logic, in a variety of languages. When you've used the business rule composer to associate business rules with the rule tasks, you can visually trace requirements all the way to code, since the business rules are propagated into the generated code as comments.

We'll show examples of automatically generated Java code, and automatically generated C# code for our Car Rental System.

Integration with IDEs—Keeping Model and Code Synchronized

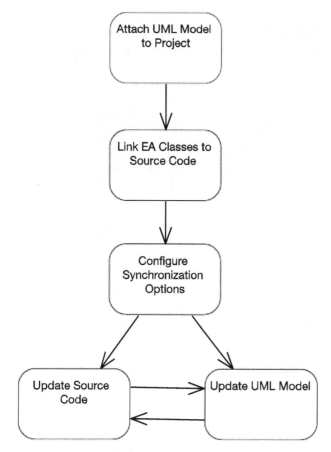

Figure 1-4. Licenses for MDG Integration for Visual Studio and Eclipse are included in the EA Business and Software Engineering Edition.

Since well before UML even existed, one of the biggest issues with modeling software has been keeping the model and the source code synchronized. The typical experience *used to be* that UML models were most useful in getting the first release of software completed, but after the initial release, the code would evolve independently in a development environment, and the UML model would rapidly grow obsolete.

With the evolution of agile methodologies, this situation often led to projects abandoning UML modeling entirely, as agile methods specify many frequent releases of the software, and getting to the first release became a smaller and smaller percentage of solving the overall problem.

We'll explain how to beat this problem entirely by using Sparx MDG Integration for Visual Studio and for Eclipse, both of which are included in the EA Business and Software Engineering Edition.

Finally, we'll demonstrate integration with Visual Studio with the C# code for our Car Rental System, and integration with Eclipse using Car Rental Java code. With that, all the steps in our roadmap for SOA development will be complete.

CHAPTER 2

Getting Organized for SOA

Before undertaking an SOA project (or any other sort of project), it's a good idea to understand some basic fundamentals about what you're planning to build. As Figure 2-1 shows, three major components of this understanding are:

- **Modeling the problem domain**
- **Identifying business rules and other requirements**
- **Storyboarding the user experience (i.e. screens)**

These elements are common to the vast majority of software systems. Once you've developed the foundation of your model, you can choose to develop various operational scenarios using web services, using normal GUI-based use cases, or to enforce business rules. In general, the web service and business rule centric scenarios "hang off" of the software use cases. So the use cases form the glue that holds the model together.

Service-oriented systems will make use of web services. In order to use web services, a system's interfaces must be defined using Web Service Definition Language (WSDL). We'll walk you through this process later in this chapter.

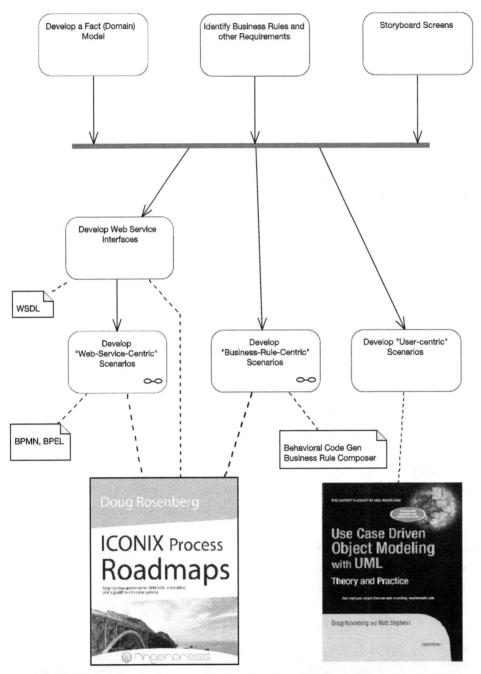

Figure 2-1. It's important to develop an understanding of the problem domain, business rules, and user experience early in the project.

Introducing the Car Rental System Example

For the remainder of this book, we'll be illustrating the SOA Roadmap using an example project—a Car Rental System. We'll use this example to illustrate developing a web service-centric scenario using BPMN/BPEL/WSDL, and we'll also use it to demonstrate the capabilities of the Sparx *Business Rule Composer* for behavioral code generation.

We'll begin with a simple domain model (also called a fact model), that shows the main objects in our problem domain. While a complete tutorial on domain modeling is out of the scope of this book, there's a full chapter devoted to this topic in *Use Case Driven Object Modeling*[49].

Figure 2-2 shows the domain model for our Car Rental System.

As you can see, the domain model establishes the vocabulary we use to describe our system, and shows relationships between objects in the problem domain. In most cases these relationships include UML generalization and aggregation relationships (not shown here).

Business Rules are represented in *Enterprise Architect* as stereotyped **Requirements**[50]. Figure 2-3 shows a Requirement Diagram for our Car Rental System that organizes these business rules according to different RuleTasks. We'll talk more about RuleTasks in Chapter 4.

---

[49] *Use Case Driven Object Modeling with UML – Theory and Practice*. Doug Rosenberg and Matt Stephens, Apress.

[50] For a tutorial on how use Enterprise Architect's relationship matrix for requirements traceability, see the Enterprise Architect for Power Users CD from ICONIX (www.iconixsw.com)

The Fact Model provides the business vocabulary - terms and facts - on which Business Rules can be modeled. In Enterprise Architect a Fact Model is created as a conceptual Class diagram.

The following diagram shows an example Fact Model, for a Car Rental system.

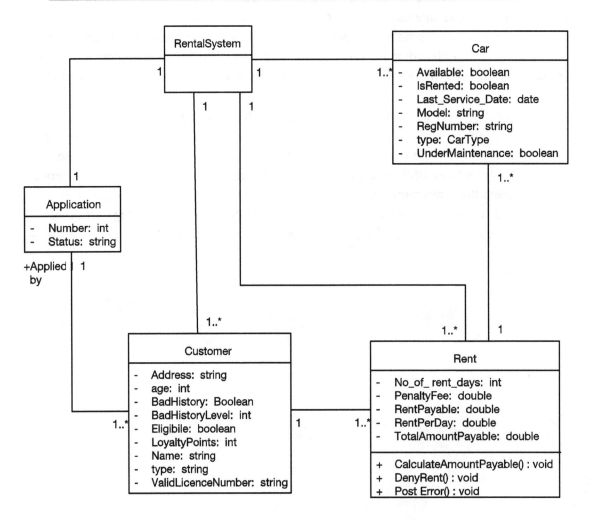

To enable a class to process the rules, right click on the appropriate class and add "Rule Flow Activity" as a behavior to the class. For this example, ProcessApplication Rule Flow Activity is added to the Rental System class.

Figure 2-2. Car Rental System Domain (Fact) Model

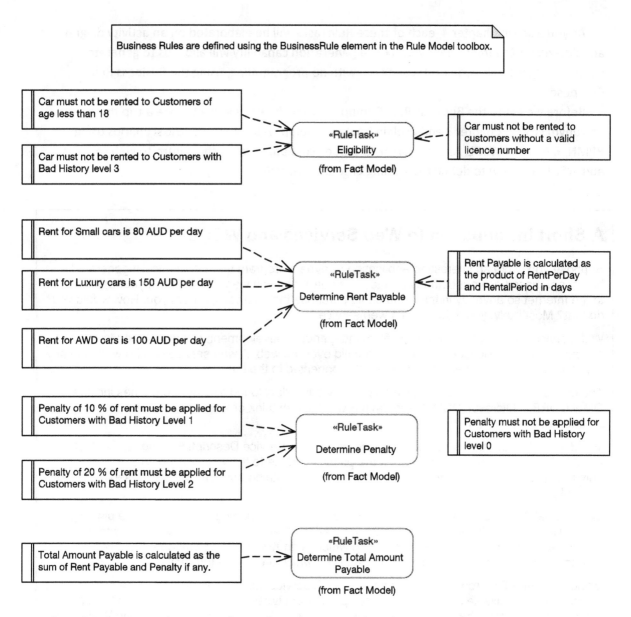

Figure 2-3. Business Rules are one flavor of Requirement, and can be organized by the RuleTask which will be responsible for enforcing the rule.

As you'll see in Chapter 4, each of these RuleTasks will be elaborated on an activity diagram, and *Enterprise Architect*'s **behavioral code generation** capability will allow us to generate complete algorithmic code for these tasks, with no programming, using the Business Rule Composer.

Before we get to the Business Rule Composer, though, we're going to take a trip through "acronym city" in Chapter 3 and explain how to develop web service-centric scenarios using BPMN, BPEL, and WSDL. As a precursor to that discussion, here's a short intro to web services and WSDL, and how to define them using *Enterprise Architect*.

A Short Introduction to Web Services and WSDL

Suppose you wrote an interesting application (maybe a program that automatically generated a horoscope based on your birthday and today's date), and you wanted to publish your application to the Internet so anybody in the world could purchase their horoscope from you. How would you do that? Most likely, you'd do it with a web service.

Web services support distributed, platform-independent development. Using web services, you can publish any application you choose to build over the web. A web service can be written in any language and hosted on any computer that's connected to the Internet.

The concept behind web services isn't new; previously developed similar approaches include OMG CORBA, Microsoft DCOM, and Java/RMI. You can think of a web service as something like an Internet-enabled API.

You'd describe your horoscope web service using Web Service Description Language (WSDL), an XML-based language that describes the public interface to the web service. WSDL tells you only how you can interact with the web service; it says nothing about how the web service works internally.

The internal details of the web service are specified using a "binding". There's a Java binding, which allows you to define local Java implementations that implement web services, and there's also SOAP (Simple Object Access Protocol) which is an XML protocol that operates over standard HTTP to communicate with web services which are on the Internet.

Using SOAP/HTTP, programs connecting to a web service can read the WSDL to determine what operations are available on the server. Any special data types used are embedded in the WSDL file as XML Schema. The program then uses SOAP to call the operations listed in the WSDL.

WSDL defines Services as collections of Network Endpoints, or Ports; a collection of Ports defines a Service. A Port associates a network address with a reusable binding, and a Message is an abstract description of the data that is being exchanged. A WSDL file has an *abstract* section that describes Ports and Messages, and a *concrete* section that describes specific instances of their usage.

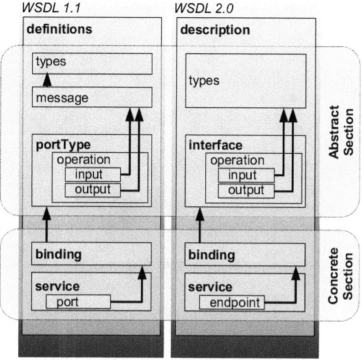

Figure 2-4. WSDL file structure showing Abstract and Concrete sections (from Wikipedia[51])

Developing Web Service Interfaces (WSDL) with Enterprise Architect

Before you can use BPMN and BPEL to orchestrate a collaborating group of web services, you first need to be able to define the web services themselves. The Business and Software Engineering Edition of *Enterprise Architect* includes a WSDL toolbox, precisely for this purpose. As you can see from Figure 2-5, the elements on this toolbox correspond to the sections in Figure 2-4.

---

[51] http://en.wikipedia.org/wiki/Web_Services_Description_Language

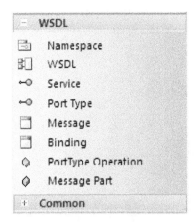

Figure 2-5. Enterprise Architect's Business and Software Engineering Edition supports WSDL development

WSDL Packages in *Enterprise Architect* are organized into **Types**, **Messages**, **Ports**, **Bindings**, and **Services** as shown in Figure 2-6.

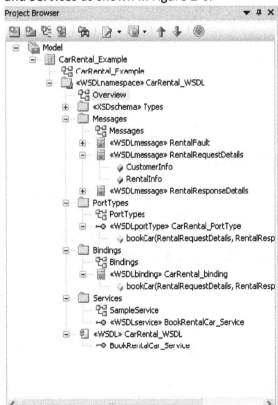

Figure 2-6. Organization of a WSDL Package in Enterprise Architect

WSDL documents are represented in Enterprise Architect by UML components stereotyped as WSDL. These components are modeled as direct child elements of the top-level WSDL namespace package. You can create multiple WSDL documents for a single namespace, thus enabling the services for that namespace to be reused and exposed as required across multiple WSDLs.

Figure 2-7 shows a WSDL component, along with the contents of Message, Port, Bindings, and Services Packages, and XSD Schema classes.

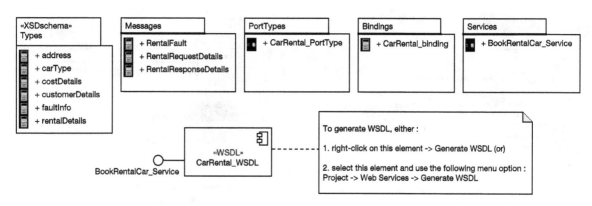

Figure 2-7. WSDL Component for CarRental, exposing the BookRentalCar Service

WSDL Bindings are represented in *Enterprise Architect* by UML classes stereotyped as WSDLbinding. Bindings should be defined under the Bindings package in the WSDL namespace structure. Each WSDLbinding class implements the operations specified by a particular WSDL portType interface. Therefore, WSDL Port Types should be defined before creating WSDL bindings.

SDL Port Types are represented in *Enterprise Architect* by UML interfaces stereotyped as WSDLportType. PortTypes should be defined under the PortTypes packages in the WSDL namespace structure. WSDL portType operations are represented in *Enterprise Architect* by operations defined as part of a WSDLportType interface.

WSDL Services are represented in *Enterprise Architect* by UML interfaces, stereotyped as WSDLservice. Services should be defined under the Services packages in the WSDL namespace structure.

WSDL Messages are represented in *Enterprise Architect* by UML classes stereotyped as WSDLmessage. Messages should be defined under the Messages package in the WSDL namespace structure. WSDL message parts are represented in *Enterprise Architect* by UML attributes defined as part of a WSDLmessage class.

Generating WSDL

Once we've defined our Bindings, Port Types, Messages, and Services, it's time to generate WSDL by right-clicking on our WSDL component and choosing Generate WSDL from the context menu. Figure 2-8 shows the WSDL generation in progress.

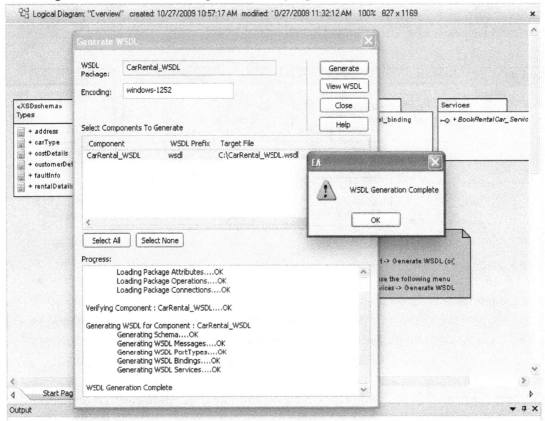

Figure 2-8. Enterprise Architect generates WSDL automatically

The result of WSDL generation for our Car Rental component can be seen in Figure 2-9.

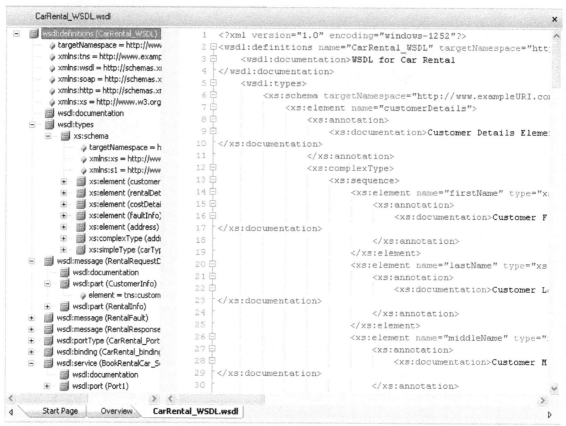

Figure 2-9. We've successfully generated WSDL for the Car Rental component

We're Ready to Go . . .

Okay, at this point we've modeled the problem domain, identified our business rules, storyboarded our screens, and defined the interfaces to our Web Services using WSDL. In Chapter 3 we'll walk through the process of orchestrating the web services to do something useful, and in Chapter 4 we'll introduce ***behavioral code generation*** and the Business Rule Composer.

CHAPTER 3

Orchestrating Web Services With BPMN and BPEL

In this chapter, we'll illustrate a "cookbook" process for developing business processes that use a group of web services collaborating to accomplish their requirements (see Figure 3-1). We'll use the BPEL language to accomplish this. BPEL is an orchestration language that describes *messages to and from a business process*. Those messages are defined using WSDL.

We'll be using the BPMN modeling notation to define our BPEL for the Car Rental system, although other notations could have been used. Let's start with an overview of BPEL.

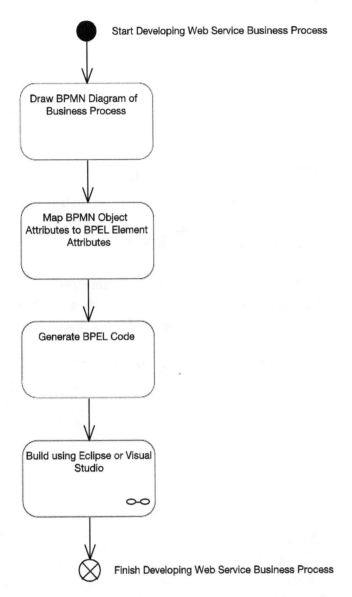

Figure 3-1. Roadmap for developing web-service centric business processes.

A Quick Overview of BPEL

BPEL is short for WS-BPEL, which is short for Web Services Business Process Execution Language. You can use BPEL to build web services, to write programs that call web services, and to describe high-level business processes that make use of web services.

BPEL business processes are often used to implement business-to-business (B2B) transactions where one business provides a web service and another business uses it. Our car rental example in this book is an example of this sort of B2B transaction.

As more and more businesses publish functionality to the Internet in the form of web services, the richness of BPEL applications, and therefore the overall importance of BPEL as a development language, will continue to increase.

BPEL is an XML-based programming language. In addition to the logic, which is described in BPEL, data types are defined using XML Schema Definitions (XSD) and input/output is described using WSDL.

BPEL is sometimes referred to as an orchestration language because it supports complex orchestrations (sequences of messages being exchanged) of multiple service applications. Orchestration refers to the central control of the behavior of a distributed system as opposed to choreography, which refers to a distributed system that operates without centralized control. BPEL's orchestration concepts are used by both the external (abstract) and internal (executable) views of a business process.

There is (intentionally) no standard graphical notation for BPEL, and as a result, some vendors have invented their own notations. However, many people use BPMN (Business Process Modeling Notation) as a graphical front-end to capture BPEL process descriptions. We'll be using BPMN to model BPEL in this book with our Car Rental example.

It has been said that BPEL is more popular among web service developers while BPMN is more popular in the business community. Some concepts in BPMN (for example, loops) were left out of BPEL to make the language easier to implement. On the other hand, BPMN only specifies the notation and lacks a complete set of semantics to specify unambiguous code generation. Thus there are some issues in round-trip engineering between BPMN and BPEL.

BPEL in Enterprise Architect

Enterprise Architect currently supports generating BPEL from executable processes. With the help of the BPMN version 1.1 Profile, *Enterprise Architect* enables you to develop BPEL diagrams quickly and simply. The BPEL facilities are provided in the form of:

- A BPEL Model Template in the Select Models dialog
- A BPEL diagram type, accessed through the New Diagram dialog
- A BPEL Process element in the BPMN 1.1 Core Toolbox pages, which acts as a container from which BPEL can be generated
- Custom dialogs for BPMN elements, highlighting the BPMN Tagged Values relevant to BPEL generation

You can create a BPEL model from the Project Browser, using the Select Model(s) (Model Wizard) dialog.

Enterprise Architect creates a standard package structure for BPEL models, which is shown in Figure 3-2. The standard structure contains the BPEL Process itself and the supporting components (SupportingElements and Participant Pools).

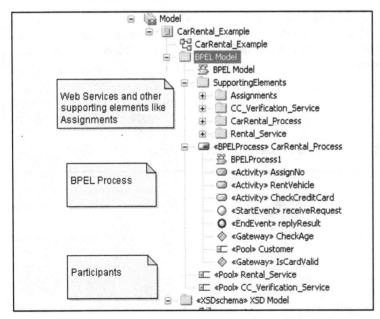

Figure 3-2. Enterprise Architect's standard BPEL Package Structure

Modeling a BPEL Process

The BPEL Process in Enterprise Architect represents the top-level container for the BPEL elements, from which BPEL can be generated. Conceptually it maps to the BPEL process element. BPEL Processes are created using the BPMN 1.1 Toolbox.

The BPEL Process element is a stereotyped Activity that, when created, has a child diagram. That diagram will contain further elements from the BPMN 1.1 Toolbox; specifically: Start Events, End Events, Intermediate Events, Gateways, Activities, Pools, and Notes.

Figure 3-3 shows the BPMN 1.1 Core Toolbox, and we'll discuss each of these elements in our BPMN tutorial, later in this chapter.

Similar to Activity Diagrams, there are 4 main categories of elements on Business Process Diagrams (BPDs): **Flow Objects** such as Events and Activities, **Connecting Objects** such as Messages and Associations, **Swimlanes**, and **other Artifacts** such as Annotations.

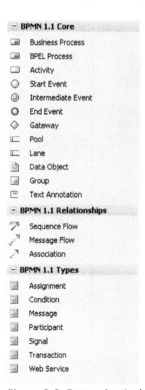

Figure 3-3. Enterprise Architect's BPMN 1.1 Core Toolbox

Note that Pools, Lanes, Data Objects, Groups, and Text Annotations are *not* mappable to BPEL.

Roadmap: Draw BPMN Diagram of Business Process

Figure 3-4 shows a BPMN diagram for our BPEL Car Rental Process. The process begins with a Start Event: a Request is received from the Customer. If the customer is of legal age to rent the vehicle, a B2B web service is used to check the Customer's credit card. If the card is valid, another web service is used to rent the vehicle, and a "Success" message is sent. If either the age or credit card checks fail, a "No" message is sent back to the customer.

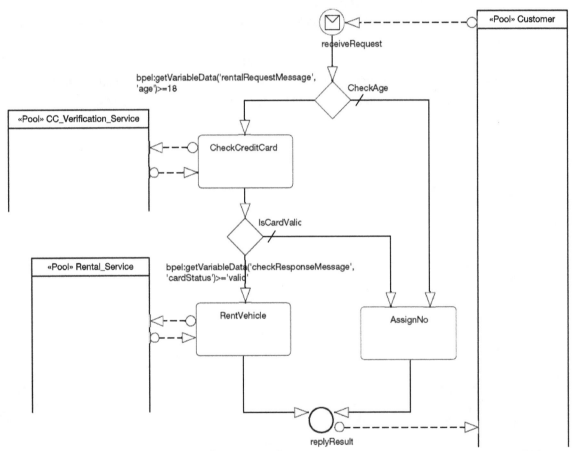

Figure 3-4. Orchestrating web services for Car Rental

Everything You Want to Know About BPMN But Were Afraid to Ask

BPMN (Business Process Modeling Notation) provides a graphical notation similar to UML activity diagrams for specifying business processes. BPMN provides a simple, standard notation that is readily understandable by analysts, developers, managers, and end-users.

BPMN is maintained by the OMG, and we'll be referring repeatedly to the "OMG BPMN 1.1 Specification" (aka "the spec") in the next couple of pages.

Start Events and End Events

A **Start Event** indicates where a particular Process begins. Every BPEL Process must begin with a Start Event. A Process can start in several ways, depending on the Trigger Type. The spec defines six types of Trigger (None, Message, Timer, Conditional, Signal, and Multiple). Four of these Trigger types (Message, Timer, Conditional, Multiple) can be mapped to BPEL.

An **End Event** indicates where a particular Process ends. A Process can start in many ways, depending on the Trigger Type, but every BPEL Process must terminate with an End Event. The spec defines eight types of End Event (or Result), which determine the consequence of reaching the End Event. These are: None, Message, Error, Cancel, Compensation, Signal, Terminate, and Multiple. Five of these Result types (Message, Error, Compensation, Terminate, Multiple) can be mapped to BPEL.

Gateways

Gateways control the way in which Sequence Flows converge and diverge within a Process. They provide a gating mechanism that either allows or blocks a Sequence Flow.
The BPMN 1.1 Spec describes four types of Gateways: **Exclusive** (XOR), **Inclusive** (OR), **Complex**, and **Parallel** (AND). Three of these Gateway types (XOR, OR, and AND) can be mapped to BPEL

An **Exclusive Gateway** represents a 'fork in the road'; that is, there can be two or more alternative paths but only one can be taken. Therefore, each path is mutually exclusive (XOR). Exclusive Gateways can be either Data-Based or Event-Based .

Data-Based Exclusive Gateway is the most common type of Exclusive Gateway, where a boolean expression is evaluated to determine the flow path.

With **Event-Based Exclusive Gateways**, the branching is based on the events (such as receiving a message) that occur at that point in the Process, rather than the evaluation of an expression. As an example, when a company receives a response from a customer, they perform one set of activities if the customer responds Yes and another set of activities if the customer responds No. The customer's response determines which path is taken. This Gateway maps to a BPEL Pick element.

With **inclusive gateways**, all the outgoing Sequence Flows with a condition that evaluates to true are taken.

The **parallel gateway** provides a mechanism to create parallel flows.

Pools

A **Pool** represents a Participant in a Process and does not map to any specific BPEL element. Enterprise Architect uses Pools to represent external Participants, with which the BPEL Process communicates. These are 'black box' pools; that is, they are abstract and do not expose any details (they do not contain any BPMN elements inside them).

Activities

An **Activity** represents work that is performed within a Process. An Activity can be modeled as a **Sub-Process** (a compound Activity that is defined as a flow of other BPMN elements) or as a **Task** (an atomic Activity that cannot be broken down into a smaller unit).

Activities - both Tasks and Sub-Processes - can also act as Looping constructs. There are two types of Looping constructs, Standard (while or until) and Multi-Instance (for each). A **Standard Loop** has a boolean Condition that is evaluated after each cycle of the loop. If the evaluation is True, then the loop continues. If Test Time is set to After, the loop is equivalent to a while loop. If Test Time is set to Before, the loop is equivalent to an until loop. A **Multi-Instance Loop** is equivalent to a for each loop and has a numeric expression as a Condition that is evaluated only once before the Activity is performed. The result of the evaluation specifies the number of times the loop is repeated.

The BPMN Specification defines three types of Sub-Process: **Embedded**, **References**, and **Reusable**. Embedded and References Sub-Process types can be mapped to BPEL.

Assignments

A BPMN **Assignment** element enables data to be copied between messages, and new data to be inserted, using expressions within a BPEL Process. A BPMN Assignment element maps to a BPEL assign activity and copies the specified value from the source to the target.

In Enterprise Architect, Assignment elements should be created in the Assignments package in SupportingElements. If they are created elsewhere, they cannot be enacted correctly.

Roadmap: Map BPMN Object Attributes to BPEL Element Attributes

Once we've defined our activities, gateways, and events on our BPMN diagram, we can specify additional BPEL details as attributes on our BPMN elements. In Figure 3-5, we're defining that the CheckCreditCard activity will be implemented as a web service, and will take a request message and generate a result response.

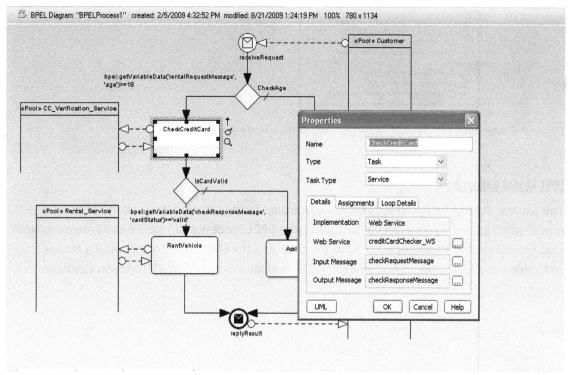

Figure 3-5. Defining Messages to and from the CheckCreditCard Web Service

In Figure 3-6, you can see that the checkRequestMessage belongs to the creditCardChecker web service, and has attributes of name and cc_details, and the checkResponseMessage has an attribute of cardStatus.

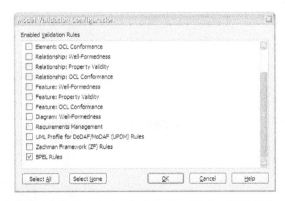

```
CarRental_Example
   CarRental_Example
   BPEL Model
      BPEL Model
      SupportingElements
         Assignments
         CC_Verification_Service
            «Participant» creditCardChecker_Participant
               «WebService» creditCardChecker_WS
                  «Message» checkRequestMessage
                     «Property» name
                     «Property» cc_details
                  «Message» checkResponseMessage
                     «Property» cardStatus
         CarRental_Process
            «Participant» carRentalFacilitator_Participant
               «WebService» carRentalFacilitator_WS
                  «Message» rentalRequestMessage
                  «Message» rentalResponseMessage
         Rental_Service
            «Participant» rentVehicle_Participant
               «WebService» rentVehicle_WS
                  «Message» rentVehicleRequestMessage
                  «Message» rentVehicleResponseMessage
      «BPELProcess» CarRental_Process
```

Figure 3-6. Messages are created inside the Web Service in the Project Browser

BPEL Model Validation

You can use Enterprise Architect's *Model Validation* facility to check the validity of the BPEL model (see Figure 3-7). You can validate an entire BPEL Process or a single BPMN element. Note that *Enterprise Architect* checks for both the UML and the BPEL rules by default. To enable only BPEL rule validation, select only the BPEL Rules checkbox in the Model Validation Configuration dialog.

Model Validation Configuration

Enabled Validation Rules

- [ ] Element: OCL Conformance
- [ ] Relationship: Well-Formedness
- [ ] Relationship: Property Validity
- [ ] Relationship: OCL Conformance
- [ ] Feature: Well-Formedness
- [ ] Feature: Property Validity
- [ ] Feature: OCL Conformance
- [ ] Diagram: Well-Formedness
- [ ] Requirements Management
- [ ] UML Profile for DoDAF/MoDAF (UPDM) Rules
- [ ] Zachman Framework (ZF) Rules
- [x] BPEL Rules

Select All   Select None   OK   Cancel   Help

Figure 3-7. Enterprise Architect validates BPEL Rules

Modeling Restrictions

Following these rules will help your BPEL modeling effort with Enterprise Architect to be more successful:

- Use the elements from the BPMN 1.1 Toolbox pages for BPEL modeling.
- Every BPEL Process and Sub-Process should start with a `StartEvent` and end with an `EndEvent`.
- A `StartEvent` or an `EndEvent` should not be attached to the boundary of a Sub-Process.
- *SequenceFlow Looping* is not supported - only Activity looping is supported. All `SequenceFlow`s should flow downstream and not upstream.
- Mapping of an `IntermediateEvent` with multiple triggers to BPEL is not supported.
- Mapping of multi-instance parallel `While` loops to BPEL is not supported.
- Mapping of Independent sub-processes to BPEL is not supported.

Generate BPEL Code

Finally, after you've specified your BPEL Process and validated the model, Enterprise Architect will generate the BPEL code to accomplish the business process (see Figure 3-8).

```
CarRental_Process.bpel                                                    ×
1    <?xml version="1.0"?>
2    <bpel:process xmlns:bpel="http://schemas.xmlsoap.org/ws/2003/03/business-process/"
3        <bpel:partnerLinks>
4            <bpel:partnerLink name="rentVehicle_Participant" partnerLinkType="crf:rentV
5            <bpel:partnerLink name="creditCardChecker_Participant" partnerLinkType="crf
6            <bpel:partnerLink name="carRentalFacilitator_Participant" partnerLinkType="
7        </bpel:partnerLinks>
8        <bpel:variables>
9            <bpel:variable name="rentalRequestMessage" messageType="crf:rentalRequestMe
10           <bpel:variable name="checkRequestMessage" messageType="cvs:checkRequestMess
11           <bpel:variable name="checkResponseMessage" messageType="cvs:checkResponseMe
12           <bpel:variable name="rentVehicleRequestMessage" messageType="crs:rentVehicl
13           <bpel:variable name="rentVehicleResponseMessage" messageType="crs:rentVehic
14           <bpel:variable name="rentalResponseMessage" messageType="crf:rentalResponse
15       </bpel:variables>
16       <bpel:sequence>
17           <bpel:receive name="receiveRequest" createInstance="yes" variable="rentalRe
18           <bpel:switch name="CheckAge">
19               <bpel:otherwise>
20                   <bpel:sequence>
21                       <bpel:sequence>
22                           <bpel:assign>
23                               <bpel:copy>
24                                   <bpel:from>not-approved</bpel:from>
25                                   <bpel:to variable="rentalResponseMessage" part="ren
26                               </bpel:copy>
27                           </bpel:assign>
28                           <bpel:empty name="AssignNo"/>
29                       </bpel:sequence>

  Start Page   BPEL Model   BPELProcess1   CarRental_Process.bpel
```

Figure 3-8. Enterprise Architect generates BPEL code from BPMN models

Once the code is generated, you're ready to move into Eclipse or Visual Studio and use the MDG Integration capability of Enterprise Architect to keep your model and the source code tightly linked together. But first, let's take a look at the Business Rule Composer and learn about *behavioral code generation*.

CHAPTER 4

Behavioral Code Generation for Business Rules

In this chapter we'll introduce you to some unique capabilities of Enterprise Architect's Business and Software Engineering Edition that provide an entirely new approach to the enforcement of business rules. Continuing our Car Rental System example, we'll show how to use Activity Diagrams to drive behavioral code generation for custom software using the Sparx Business Rule Composer.

Figure 4-1 shows our roadmap for "business rule centric" processes.

Behavioral Code Generation Includes Logic, Not Just Class Headers

For more than 20 years now, modeling tools have "generated code" from graphical models. Traditionally, this form of code generation has involved taking class definitions and generating headers, with UML attributes and operations turned into data members and function members. With the introduction of Behavioral Code Generation (which works from Activity, State, and Sequence diagrams), Sparx Systems has opened a new chapter on this technology. **It's now possible to generate complete algorithmic logic from the model**.

While *Enterprise Architect*'s behavioral code generator works with State and Sequence diagrams, the example in this chapter focuses on generating code from Activity Diagrams, specifically to implement business rules. The code generation shown in this chapter does not involve a scenario that includes a GUI—it's "pure" algorithmic code.

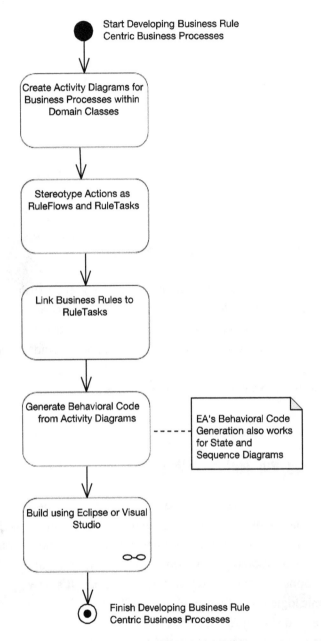

Figure 4-1. Use Activity Diagrams to model "business-rule centric" processes.

Roadmap: Create Activity Diagrams for Business Processes, within Domain Classes; Stereotype Actions as Rule Tasks

Let's look at how to process an application for our Car Rental System. The first thing to do is create a RuleFlow diagram—in this case ProcessApplication. We'll create this diagram inside of a class in the Fact Model, just as if we were creating an Operation on that class, since that is, in effect, what we're doing (see Figure 4-2).

Figure 4-2. RuleFlow diagrams are created inside Fact Model Classes.

Once we've created the RuleFlow diagram, we'll populate it with Actions, Decisions, etc. We'll stereotype these Actions as <RuleTask>s. If you recall from Chapter 2, we organized our Business Rules by RuleTask. Figure 4-3 shows the result.

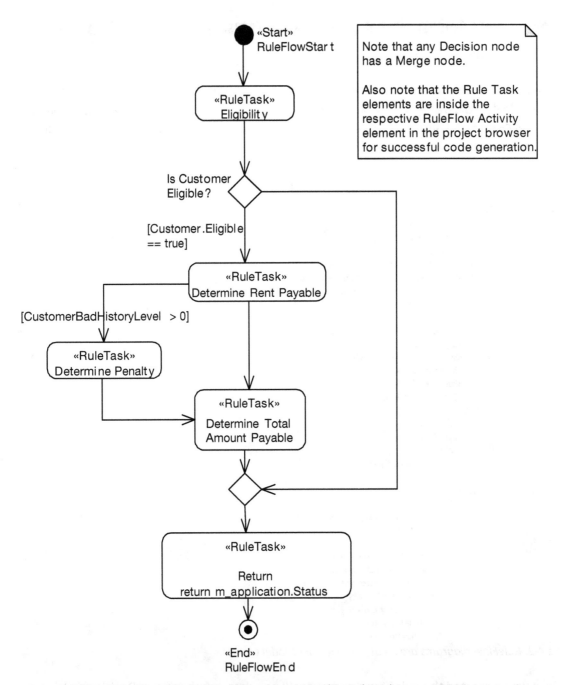

Figure 4-3. RuleFlow diagrams contain Actions stereotyped as RuleTask.

Modeling Tip:

The Rule Flow diagram models the sequence in which a series of Rule Tasks are executed. To view the Rule Composer right click on the Rule Task and select "Rule Composer" option. The conceptual level of business rules are modeled in the Rule Composer to a logical level of detail.

Our algorithm first determines whether the Customer is Eligible to rent the vehicle, then determines the price, including any possible penalties due to the Customer's history, and returns, presenting a pass/fail application status.

Roadmap: Link Business Rules to RuleTasks

Next, we should specify the conditional logic for each of these RuleTasks, while associating each RuleTask with the specific Business Rules that we're enforcing. As you might have guessed by now, that's where the Business Rule Composer comes into play. Once we've completely specified each RuleTask, we'd like Enterprise Architect to generate 100% complete code for the entire RuleFlow (Activity Diagram). Using Behavioral Code Generation, that's exactly what we'll do.

Figure 4-4 shows the Business Rule Composer for the Eligibility RuleTask.

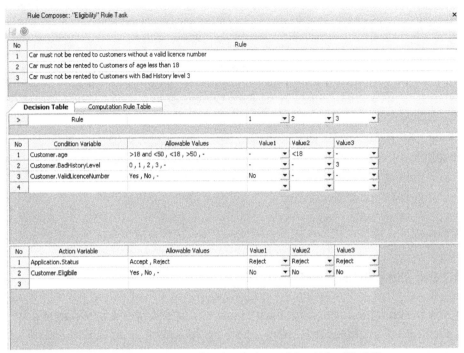

Figure 4-4. Business Rule Composer showing Rules and Logic for Eligibility.

There are 2 sections on the Rule Composer screen. The top panel shows the Business Rules (from Chapter 2) that we're satisfying within this Eligibility RuleTask; the lower section (in this case a Decision Table) has 3 parts: a Condition section to model condition variables, an Action section to model action variables, and a Rule Bind section to link the rule in the rule table.

Modeling Condition Variables

To model condition variables, we'll make use of attributes of classes that are defined in the Fact Model. We can drag and drop the required attributes from the Project Browser onto the Condition Variable column. In Figure 4-4 above, we've dragged the `age`, `BadHistoryLevel`, and `ValidLicenceNumber` attributes from the `Customer` class into the "Action Variable" column.

Next, we'll define a range of accepted values for each attribute (such as allowable `Customer.age` values being between greater than 18). A new constraint, `AllowableValues`, is created for the attribute. You can check this constraint by opening the Properties dialog for the attribute and selecting the Constraints tab. If the condition variable references an enumeration, the enum literals are not editable in the Edit Allowable Values dialog.

Modeling Action Variables

In the Action Variable section, when a specific value of a condition variable calls an operation or decision attribute you assign the operation or attribute as an action.

To model action variables, drag and drop the required attribute or operation from a Fact Model Class in the Project Browser onto the Action Variable field. For an attribute, right click on the Allowable Values field and type the range of values in the text box (e.g. Accept, Reject for Application.Status in Figure 4-4). Select the appropriate response in the Value column fields. If the dropped action variable is of type enum, the Allowable Values fields are automatically set with the enum literals. For an operation, a checkbox displays in each of the Value column fields.

Binding Business Rules to Conditions

The **Rule Bind** section lies on top of the Condition section. It binds the condition variable and action variable values to the appropriate rule in the Rule Table.

To bind a rule, follow these steps:

- Select the rule number in the Rule field over one of the Value columns
- Ensure that the values set in the Value<n> field for the condition variables and action variables, underneath the rule number, all satisfy the rule
- Click the Save button

In Figure 4-4, Rule 1 specifies that a ***Car must not be rented to Customers of age less than 18***:

- Select 1 in the Rule field over the Value1 column
- Select < 18 against Customer.age in the Value1 column in the Condition table
- Select No against Customer.Eligible in the Value1 column in the Action table
- Select Reject against Application.Status in the Value1 column in the Action table
- Select the checkbox against Rent.PostError in the Value1 column in the Action table.

Figure 4-5 shows the rules and logic for determining penalties based on the Customer's history.

Modeling Computational Rules

The Computational Rule table enables you to model rules involving computations. The table has three following columns: Rule Variable Expression, Rule, and Rule Dependency.

To define a computational rule, follow these steps:

1. Drag and drop the appropriate attribute from a Class in the Fact model into the Variable field
2. Type the expression to be evaluated
3. Type the rule number from the Rule table of the rule being modeled, to link the table data to the rule

Figure 4-6 shows an example of using the Computational Rule Table.

Combining Decision Tables and Computational Rules

It's possible to use the Decision Table and Computational Rule Table together, as shown in Figures 4-7 and 4-8.

If the rule depends on another rule being satisfied first, type the number of that rule in the Rule Dependency field. If the computation rule is also a conditional rule, add the condition variable in the Decision table and bind the appropriate rule in the Rule Bind section.

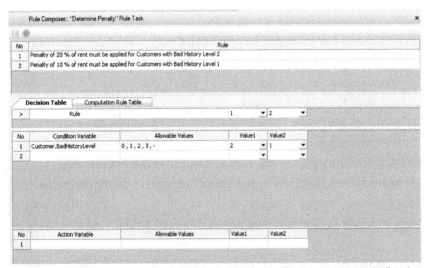

Figure 4-5. Rule Composer being used to specify the "Determine Penalty" RuleTask.

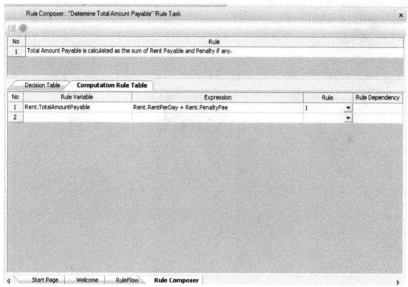

Figure 4-6. Computational Rule Table for determining Total Amount Payable.

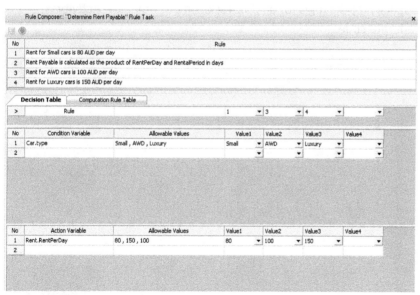

Figure 4-7. Decision Table for Determining Rent Payable.

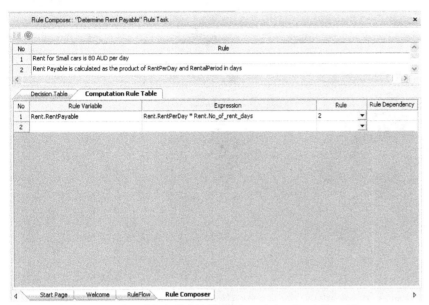

Figure 4-8. Computational Rule Table for Determining Rent Payable.

Once we've completed specifying the logic for all RuleTasks on our RuleFlow Activity Diagram, we're ready to generate code.

Roadmap: Generate Behavioral Code from Activity Diagrams

Code generation turns out to be very simple (and yields astonishing results) once all the preliminary work has been done. Simply right-click on the Fact Model Class in the Project Browser and select "Generate Code"... and... Voila! No programming required!

```
       RentalSystem.cs
 ⊟  RentalSystem           31      public bool ProcessApplication(Rent m_rent, Application m_application)
        m_Car               32      {
        m_Customer          33          // behavior is a Activity
        m_Rent              34
        Dispose()           35              /*CAR MUST NOT BE RENTED TO CUSTOMERS WITHOUT A VALID LICENCE NUMBER*
        ProcessApplication()36              if( m_Customer.ValidLicenceNumber == "FALSE" )
        RentalSystem()      37              {
        ~RentalSystem()     38                  m_application.Status = "Reject";
                            39                  m_Customer.Eligibile = false;
                            40              }
                            41              /*CAR MUST NOT BE RENTED TO CUSTOMERS OF AGE LESS THAN 18*/
                            42              if( m_Customer.age < 18 )
                            43              {
                            44                  m_application.Status = "Reject";
                            45                  m_Customer.Eligibile = false;
                            46              }
                            47              /*CAR MUST NOT BE RENTED TO CUSTOMERS WITH BAD HISTORY LEVEL 3*/
                            48              if( m_Customer.BadHistoryLevel == 3 )
                            49              {
                            50                  m_application.Status = "Reject";
                            51                  m_Customer.Eligibile = false;
                            52              }
                            53          if (Customer.Eligible == true)
                            54          {
                            55
                            56                  /*RENT FOR SMALL CARS IS 80 AUD PER DAY*/
                            57                  if( m_Car.type == Small )
                            58                  {
                            59                      m_rent.RentPerDay = 80;
                            60                  }
                            61                  /*RENT FOR AWD CARS IS 100 AUD PER DAY*/
                            62                  if( m_Car.type == AWD )
                            63                  {
```

Figure 4-9. 100% complete logic, with Business Rules appearing as comments within the code!

It's worth examining the code shown in Figure 4-9 quite carefully. Here are a few points worth noting:

- **The entire** `RuleFlow` **diagram is code generated as if it were a single class** `Operation` **on the** `FactModel` **Class**
- **Each** `RuleTask` **is expanded in turn**
- **Within each** `RuleTask`**, the Business Rules are automatically propagated forward into the code as comments**
- **Attribute and Operation names are taken directly from the Rule Composer**
- **No manual programming intervention is required**

It doesn't take a whole lot of imagination to see that this capability can be a real "game-changer". Many organizations have thousands of business rules to implement, and "errors in translation" between subject matter experts, business analysts and programmers are the norm, not the exception. Many of those errors can be eliminated using Behavioral Code Generation and the Business Rule Composer.

There's one more step in our Roadmap for "business-rule centric" processes, and that's the process of building the system in either Eclipse or Visual Studio. That's the subject of the next chapter.

CHAPTER 5

Integrating Models and Code

EA contains numerous features to help with code generation and reverse engineering, and also integrates closely with the *Visual Studio* and *Eclipse* development environments via its MDG Integration technology. Many of EA's code engineering capabilities, including forward and reverse engineering, and EA's powerful code template framework, are described in detail in the Enterprise Architect for Power Users multimedia tutorial.[52] This chapter will focus in on the MDG Integration capability.

Mind the Reality Gap

Since the beginning of modeling time, the gap (sometimes a chasm) between models and code has always been problematic. Models, the argument goes, don't represent reality... only the code represents reality... therefore the model must be worthless, and we should just skip modeling and jump straight to code. Those who have used this argument to avoid modeling probably felt quite safe in doing so because nobody has ever managed to make "reverse engineering" or "round-trip engineering" a very seamless process... until now. The innocuously named "MDG Integration" product changes the whole equation.

---

[52] See: http://iconixsw.com/EA/PowerUsers.html

Bringing Mohammed to the mountain

You can lead some programmers to UML, but you can't always make them embrace modeling. The ever-present gap between models and code is one of the reasons for this. Modeling introduces another environment, another tools interface, another user interface to learn, and forces the programmer to leave the familiar confines of his or her coding environment, where he has all the comforts of home.

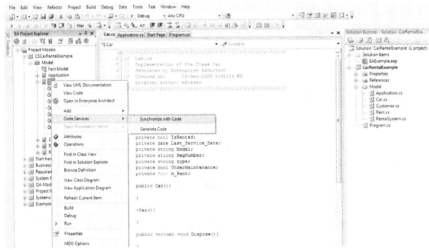

Figure 5-1. Bringing the UML model inside the IDE (in this case, Visual Studio) has many benefits.

But what would happen if the UML model was brought inside of the programming environment? (See Figure 5-1). Let's say if you could open your project, right click a menu, and say something like "Attach UML Model". So you can browse your use cases, sequence diagrams, classes, etc from within *Visual Studio* or *Eclipse*.

Then let's suppose you could hot link a package of classes from the UML window to the source code. Nice, but not compelling yet? How's this? You can double-click an operation on a class in the UML window and instantly browse to the source code for that method, and you can edit the code as you normally would in *Visual Studio* or *Eclipse* and update the UML model by right-clicking on the class and choosing *Synchronize*.

Suddenly, the UML model is actually helping you to navigate through your code, you can click to see the use cases and sequence diagrams that are using the classes you're building, and you can re-synch the models effortlessly. Suddenly your UML model is the asset that it was supposed to be all along.

But... here's the six million dollar question: **how do you keep the model and the code synchronized over the lifetime of the project?**

Four Simple Steps to Modeling Nirvana—without chanting OMMMMM

A few years ago, Matt Stephens and I wrote a whole chapter in *Agile Development with ICONIX Process*[53] about how to synchronize models and code, and the reasons why it's important. Synchronizing models and code is still just as important, but the folks at Sparx Systems have obsoleted the "how-to" guidance from that chapter. Now it's absurdly simple. So simple that an old tool-builder like me wonders "why the heck didn't I think of that?"

Here's how it works:

1. Connect your UML model to a Visual Studio or Eclipse project
2. Link a package in the model to classes within the IDE
3. Browse the source code by clicking on operations on classes
4. Edit the source code in your IDE

EA keeps your model and code synchronized, automatically, or you can force synchronization at any time by selecting *Synchronize from Code* from the *Code Services* menu as shown in Figure 5-2.

Figure 5-2. Java code and UML model for our Car Rental example shown in Eclipse

---

[53] See www.iconixsw.com/Books.html for more on the Agile/ICONIX process.

Wrapping Up

That completes our roadmap for developing Service Oriented Architecture projects using the Enterprise Architect Business and Software Engineering Edition. Our roadmap has taken us from Requirements definition, through implementation of web-service centric scenarios using BPMN, BPEL, and WSDL, business-rule centric scenarios using Behavioral Code Generation and the Business Rule Composer, and finally covered how to effortlessly synchronize UML models and source code over the lifetime of your projects.

We wish you success in your development efforts!

APPENDIX A

Bonus Roadmap: Design Driven Testing for Systems

By Doug Rosenberg—many thanks to Michael Sievers at the Jet Propulsion Laboratory (Pasadena, CA) for his valuable inputs.

Design Driven Testing (DDT) was first outlined in the book *Use Case Driven Object Modeling with UML: Theory and Practice* (by Doug Rosenberg and Matt Stephens), and then described in detail in *Design Driven Testing: Test Smarter, Not Harder* by the same authors. Although DDT can be successfully used in conjunction with Test Driven Development (TDD), it really follows the opposite development philosophy: starting with a design (and requirements and use cases) and driving tests from them.

DDT is a highly methodical approach to testing, allowing you to know when you've finished—i.e. when you've written enough tests to cover the design and the requirements. It helps you to "zoom in" and write algorithmic tests to cover intensive or mission-critical sections of code, and to know when it's safe to "zoom out" and write fewer tests for boilerplate or less critical code. Consequently you tend to end up with fewer tests overall than with TDD—but comparatively more test *scenarios* per test case.

In this Appendix, Doug extends the concept of DDT for hardware/software systems, allowing SysML-based designs to be tested in a highly rigorous, systematic way. It's still Design Driven Testing, but now the design elements that need to be tested include all of the "four pillars of SysML", whereas DDT for software focuses on testing behavior.

Doug (not being an actual rocket scientist) would like to acknowledge some informal but very valuable and entertaining discussions with Dr. Michael Sievers of NASA's Jet Propulsion Laboratory (JPL) regarding how real rocket scientists would approach the problem of detecting potholes from outer space—and how they would test their designs.

Introduction

This Appendix discusses an integrated, model-based design approach based on an extension of Design Driven Testing (DDT)[54] that is compatible with Validation & Verification (V&V) activities at all design levels. **(We define V&V in the sidebar on Page 216)**. Models are validated at each step and the validated models are then used for verification tests. Essentially the design is the model and the model is the design. At some level of detail the "model" is physical hardware and executable software and the V&V process uses familiar unit, bench, and integration tests.

While DDT is related to software simulations currently used in the industry, it differs in at least one key aspect: typically software simulations are built by independent teams from independent requirements. There is always a question of how close the software simulation is to the real system. In our approach, there is one system model which may be viewed in different ways and at different levels of detail as suits a user's needs. Moreover, as will be seen in the Design Driven Testing section, our approach guides "smart" selection of test cases which saves cost and schedule. This is particularly important because while systems have become more complex, the time allocated for testing has not changed. We must now test more, but in the same amount of time as simpler systems. This can only become practical by improving test efficiency.

DDT is intimately linked to modern, model-based systems engineering using the SysML paradigm. Like SysML which establishes a single, common source for design truth, DDT provides a single, consistent source of V&V truth and establishes clear lines of responsibility. Equally important is that DDT is integrated with the iterative design process assuring that each level of design is consistent with its parent and children.

---

[54] *Design Driven Testing: Test Smarter, Not Harder* by Matt Stephens and Doug Rosenberg (Apress, 2010).

ROCKET SCIENCE:
Why Use a Space Mission to Illustrate DDT/Systems?

A space mission is a system of interacting systems that implement a set of behaviors defined by operational concepts. Operations concepts describe all phases of the mission from ground-based testing through pre-launch, launch, separation, commissioning, nominal operations and eventually disposal or decommissioning. Each of these "use cases" comprises complex actions, alternate paths and exceptional conditions. When a typical mission costs taxpayers hundreds of millions to billions of dollars, it is crucial that these systems are validated and verified from the highest conceptual levels down to the detailed code that defines the functions in an FPGA. The cost of finding and fixing problems escalates by orders of magnitude as the mission progresses through its design and deployment stages hence, systematic and early Validation and Verification (V&V) are central aspects of all space programs.

A Model System Design

Using SysML, we describe the design of a fanciful, yet somewhat realistic spacecraft mission for a running example in this paper. The next section discusses the system V&V process as an extension to DDT. We then illustrate the system V&V method applied to our spacecraft design.

Our mission goal is a system that images the city streets it passes over with a sufficiently large telescope that it can resolve large street imperfections. We call our spacecraft: Persistent Open Traffic Hazard Obstacles, Large and Elongated (POTHOLE) because all spacecraft must have a clever name. POTHOLE sends images to the ground where they are processed and new or growing potholes can be reported to local maintenance bureaus.

Figure A-1 shows a conceptual diagram of POTHOLE spacecraft. Major visible components are the solar array in green, telescope in dark blue, sunshade in light blue, downlink antenna in silver and the "Bus" in yellow. The Bus consists of the functions needed to maintain the vehicle and communicate with the ground. The telescope and related imaging functions are collectively called the "Instrument." The mission block diagram in Figure 3 shows that the POTHOLE spacecraft is a composition of the Bus and Instrument systems. The mission also requires a Ground Station for controlling the spacecraft and accepting and processing images.

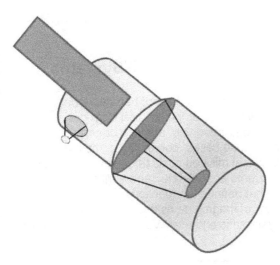

Figure A-1. POTHOLE Spacecraft

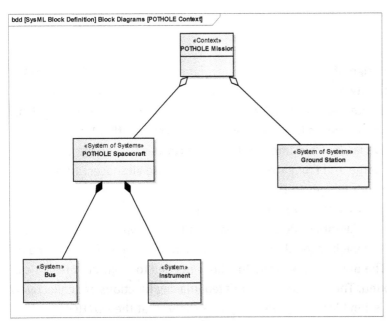

Figure A-2. POTHOLE Mission Block Diagram

We next define a few key business requirements constituting the contract between the customer and the implementer. Business rules define the constraints and functions that must be delivered by the implementer and are the basis for the customer's acceptance criteria.

ROCKET SCIENCE: V&V Challenges

Several challenges are inherent in current V&V methodologies.

• There are multiple layers of requirements (refer to Figure A-3)—mission, systems, subsystems, assemblies, units and components.

• Mission requirements are often driven by capabilities. Instead of asking, "What do you want us to build?" we are often asked, "What do you have and how can we use it?"

• A design is V&V'd through tests, analysis, demonstration and inspection.

• Keeping track of who does what and how lower level V&V rolls up into higher levels is not managed very well.

• Tests at higher levels wait until tests at lower levels have completed. So problems related to validating higher level functions aren't recognized until later in the development cycle when it is more expensive and time consuming to fix them.

• Models (e.g. aerothermal and reliability models) are often used for various aspects of V&V. These models are not integrated and do not necessarily provide an easy path for incorporating effects in one model into another.

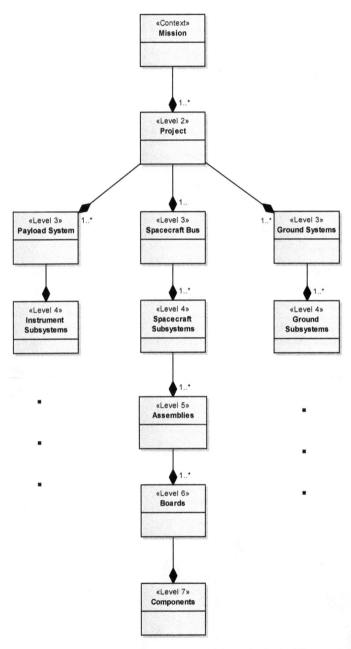

Figure A-3. Typical space system design hierarchy includes up to seven levels of specification and V&V

POTHOLE Business Requirements

Figure A-4 shows the ten requirements, as modeled in Enterprise Architect. Mission requirements derive from the opportunities and limitations in system use, environmental conditions, functional criticality, and the other systems the customer employs in support of the system.

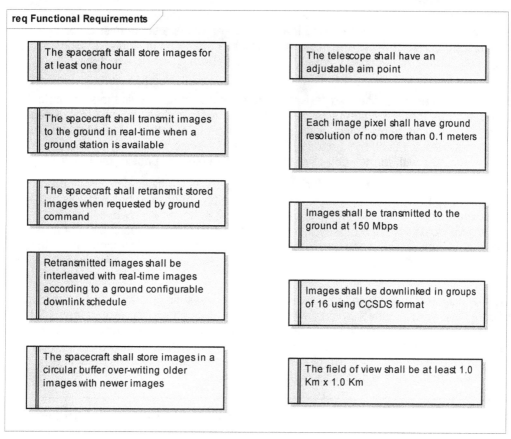

Figure A-4. POTHOLE Mission Requirements

ROCKET SCIENCE: Validation and Verification (V&V)

We define **validation** as the processes performed to assure that we are building the right thing for specified needs. If a user wants to measure magnetic fields around a planet then our design must include a magnetometer. We should not build our spacecraft with something else unless we have discussed it with our customers and they agree that our alternative is acceptable. In a space flight mission, validation focuses on certifying that the system meets a set of mission objectives documented in operations concepts and mission plans while operating in flight-like conditions. Validation is often subjective because it asks whether the system is able to accomplish its mission goals.

Verification is defined as the processes performed that assure we have built the system right. Verification determines that the system has the right components to do its job and that at each level of design those components satisfy a set of requirements. Collectively, requirements are a formal contract between the customers and implementers of a system. Unlike validation, verification is associated with formal, objective tests that have either a pass or fail result.

Defining comprehensive yet efficient V&V for complex systems is a difficult problem and is often made more difficult by fuzzy requirements, incomplete definition of desired behaviors, multiple teams, and unclear responsibilities. Inefficient V&V resulting in unnecessary overlaps or repeated tests adds costs time and money but is far less dangerous than incomplete or missing tests. Yet testing all combinations and permutations of a complex system is impossible both for the size of the problem and for the lack of visibility into internal operations as systems are integrated.

Typically, a space system is designed top-down and bottom-up. Mission planners think through the type of data they want to collect which drives lower-level allocations and requirements. At the same time, designers are often looking at what hardware and software they can reuse even though they may not yet have a complete understanding of what functions they must provide. Often bottom-up selection and top-down mission analyses and decompositions meet in a integration and test facility where disconnects are frequently found.

The Bus and Instrument structures are further detailed in the block definition diagrams (BDDs) shown in Figures A-5 and A-6 respectively.

There are six major subsystems that form the Bus: Telecom which consists of radios for ground communication. Guidance and Navigation is responsible for know where the vehicle is relative to the ground and for maintaining pointing so that the telescope points to the Earth's surface while the solar array points to the sun. Avionics houses the flight computers on which flight software executes. The Propulsion subsystem includes the thrusters, valves, and propulsion tanks. Temperatures are maintained by the Thermal subsystem and the Power subsystem manages electrical power.

Lunchtime Conversation with a Rocket Scientist

We discussed our fictitious mission requirements with a friendly rocket scientist over lunch. The conversation went something like this:

Well, the first requirement tells us how long we have to keep images onboard. Once we know the image capture rate and image size, we can place a lower bound on how much storage we need. The seventh requirement tells us that our field of view (FOV) is 1.0 Km x 1.0 Km. Assuming we want to take an image in every 1.0 Km x 1.0 Km patch, then we have to take an image every time the ground track of the spacecraft moves 1.0 Km which can be computed from the spacecraft orbit (inclination and altitude).

Pizza arrives…

For example, at an altitude of 20,000 Km (GPS altitude), we need to image roughly every 100 milliseconds at the equator. Requirement 9 tells us that our image sensor is 10K pixels * 10K pixels = 100M pixels. At 12 bits per pixel, each image is 1.2 Gb. Storing images for an hour translates into around 4.3Tb of onboard storage—a large number, but still within the realm of current solid state recorder technology.

Time for a second slice…

In a real design, we would be quite concerned about the practicalities of building a telescope and optics with the required precision. However, for our purposes, we are only interested in data collection, transport, and processing. Our back-of-the-envelope analysis gives us interface rates, storage requirements, image sensor size, and hints of needed processing throughput. We're now ready to define our domain model and use cases.

The Instrument comprises Data Storage for holding images when ground stations are not in view and for retransmission, a Camera that takes images, an Instrument Computer that manages the instrument and image collection functions, and the Telescope which consists of mirrors and optics.

Figure A-7 is an IBD that shows interfaces between the CDH processor, Local Engineering Unit (LEU) used for analog data sampling, Non-Volatile Memory (NVM) used to store critical variables and software images, and the Communications Interface (CommInterface) that sends and receives messages from the telecom radios. We use the highlighted NVM to define interface tests in the validation section below.

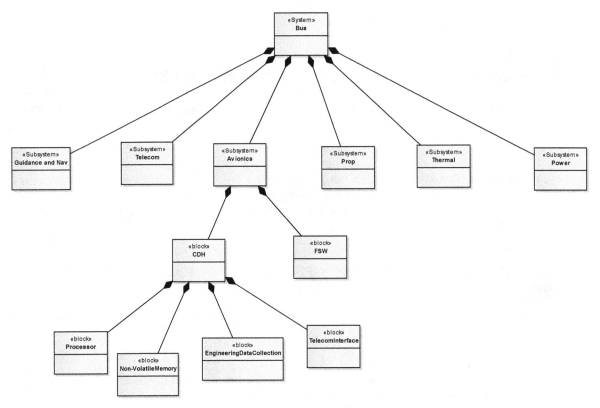

Figure A-5. POTHOLE Spacecraft Bus BDD

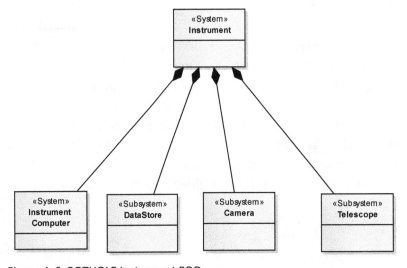

Figure A-6. POTHOLE Instrument BDD

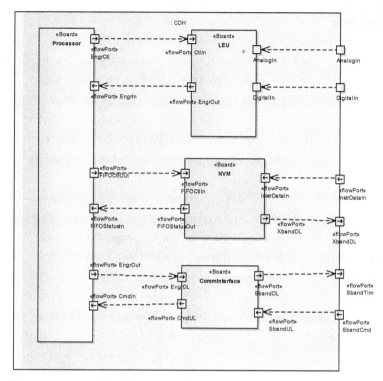

Figure A-7. Examples of CDH interfaces

Earlier we made a case for top-down and integrated V&V, yet here we are showing significant detail for our hypothetical spacecraft. Natural questions might be: how did we come to this partitioning, how do we know it is right, and could there be a better decomposition that does what we need? The simple answer is that these are basic functions of a 3-axis stabilized spacecraft that can capture images and send them to the ground. Within this structure designers are free to allocate specific behaviors and requirements. Moreover, we are free to modify the structure if our V&V process determines that it is not adequate.

Why distinguish between "Bus," and "Instrument," couldn't these be just part of a Flight Vehicle and avoid the intermediate partition? The Bus and Instrument partitions are neither required nor necessary but reflect the reality that different development groups are usually responsible for providing Bus and Instrument functions. These groups independently design and test their portion of the spacecraft and then eventually those systems are brought together and tested. This highlights the point made earlier that traditional V&V waits for verification of lower level functions before testing higher level functions. Electrical and functional interface documents define how this should happen and when everything is properly specified and implemented then all works out. But, that's not always the case.

POTHOLE Domain and Use Case Models

We have a good idea of what behaviors are needed in the POTHOLE spacecraft for collecting and transmitting images to the ground for pothole analysis. Those behaviors also help define our domain model. Domain models and use cases are tightly coupled because use cases refer to domain elements and domain elements must be present in at least one use case. Consequently, domain and use case model interactions are the basis of initial model validation because each model checks the other. Neither model can be considered complete or correct unless each is consistent with and supportive of the other.

From the requirements and mission goal, we know that our domain model must have an "image" element. We also know that individual images are packaged on the spacecraft prior to downlink, so our domain needs a concept of "image collection" which is composed of "images." Similarly, we know that we will need some sort of "image queue" in our domain model that feeds images to analysis software because images cannot be processed concurrently.

The domain model in Figure A-8 and the corresponding use case model in Figure A-9 result from iterating domain elements and use case descriptions. Figure A-8 populates model elements with conceptual function definitions. These may need revision as more detail is known, but at this point, the elements and functions are consistent with the use cases in Figure A-9 and the mission requirements.

The domain model includes the Instrument that produces an Image Collection which is created as an aggregation of individual Images. The Image Collection has an association with the Ground Station through the Telecom subsystem. The Ground Station maintains an Image Queue for analyzing and annotating the Images. Images annotated with Potholes are sent to the Subscriber by the ground station.

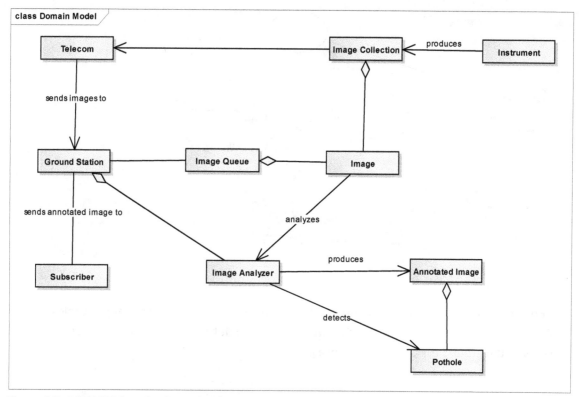

Figure A-8. POTHOLE Imaging Domain Diagram

The mission-level use cases for our reference function shown in Figure A-9 complement the domain model and reflect our understanding of the imaging collection and analysis process. The spacecraft must achieve and maintain the correct orbit (Maintain Orbit). The instrument must be aimed at a point on the ground point prior to looking for potholes (Aim Instrument). Spacecraft health must be maintained throughout the mission (Maintain Spacecraft Health) including dealing with spacecraft emergencies (entering safemode which keeps the spacecraft power positive and in communication with the ground). When commanded, we capture and process images (Look for Potholes) and if images are corrupted in transmission, the ground may request that they be retransmitted (Retransmit Images).

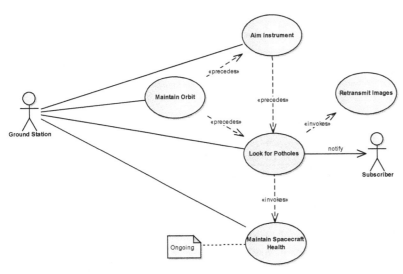

Figure A-9. POTHOLE Mission-Level Use Cases

Because our primary mission is pothole detection, we focus on the "Look for Potholes" scenario that collects images with sufficient resolution to detect large potholes and sends the images to the ground for processing. More precisely:

```
Basic Course:

Ground Station sends a command to Spacecraft to collect Images.
Instrument collects Images, resulting in an Image Collection
Telecom sends the Image Collection to the Ground Station
Ground Station adds Images to Image Queue
Image Analyzer gets Image from Image Queue
Image Analyzer detects Potholes and produces Annotated Image showing Pothole
locations
Image Analyzer sends Annotated Image to Subscriber


Alternate Courses:

Ground Station sends a command to Spacecraft to retransmit Image Collection:
Invoke Retransmit Images
Spacecraft enters safemode: invoke Maintain Spacecraft Health
Ground Station sends a command to Spacecraft to stop collecting images: invoke
Maintain Spacecraft Health
```

A few things are worth pointing out in this "ICONIX process style" use case[55]. The scenario is written precisely using nouns (shown in bold) that represent objects in the domain or context models. Verbs apply actions that transform one noun into another noun or transport a noun to another action. Bold italicized text refers to use cases in the use case diagram.

Comparing the nouns and verbs in our use case with the domain model elements gives us confidence that our models are consistent. But we don't yet know that we defined the use case scenario correctly and so we can't yet claim that we have validated our initial concepts. Our next step creates a conceptual design in the form of a robustness diagram[56] that facilitates a design walk-through for validating the use cases. We will see later that the robustness diagram is also an essential tool for defining test cases.

POTHOLE Conceptual Design

Figure A-10 shows a robustness diagram for the Look for Potholes use case. In a robustness diagram, the logical and conceptual structures are analyzed ensuring that the use cases it models are sufficiently robust for the intended usage behaviors and requirements. Robustness diagrams are annotated with requirements establishing completeness and consistency design. Missing, incorrect, and incomplete requirements become readily apparent.

A robustness diagram comprises: actors (people or external systems that interact with the system under consideration, boundaries (interfaces that actors interact with), controllers (the verbs in the use case statements), and entities (elements from the domain or context models).

A few simple interaction rules define the construction of robustness diagrams:

- Entities and controllers may interact.
- Actors and boundaries may interact.
- Boundaries and controllers may interact.
- Entities cannot directly interact with other entities.

In Figure A-10, circles with arrows represent controllers, underlined circles are entities and circles attached to vertical lines are boundaries. Requirements are associated with controllers. Every controller must have at least one requirement so Figure A-10 is not complete. Moreover,

---

[55] *Use Case Driven Object Modeling with UML: Theory and Practice* by Doug Rosenberg and Matt Stephens.

[56] Ivar Jacobson, et. al. (1992), *Object Oriented Software Engineering - A Use Case Driven Approach*, Addison Wesley.

223

every requirement must be associated with a controller and missing associations mean either omissions in the robustness diagram or unnecessary requirements.

We can walk through the *Look for Potholes* steps and follow the flow in the robustness diagram. Inconsistencies are reconciled by altering robustness elements to reflect the use cases it represents and/or changing the use cases to mirror the robustness diagram. Since updates to use cases may also cause domain model revisions, when iterations are complete, the robustness, use case, and domain models are self-consistent.

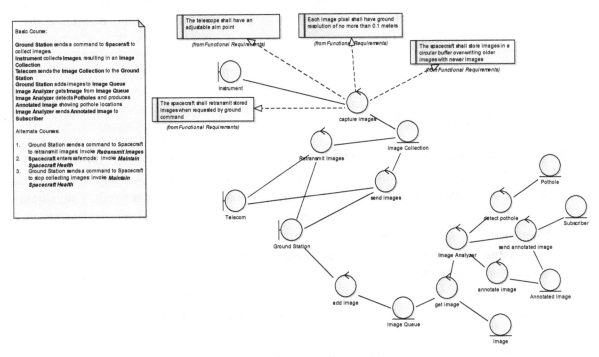

Figure A-10. POTHOLE Robustness Diagram with a few example requirements

Figure A-11 shows a portion of the sequence diagram associated with the Look for Potholes use case. Behaviors are allocated to the system elements defined in the domain model and block diagrams. Each behavior must be unit tested, as shown in Figure A-25.

The Extended Domain Model in Figure A-12 shows an object-oriented allocation of behavior to system elements. Allocations satisfy all behaviors specified in the use case as shown in the sequence diagram.

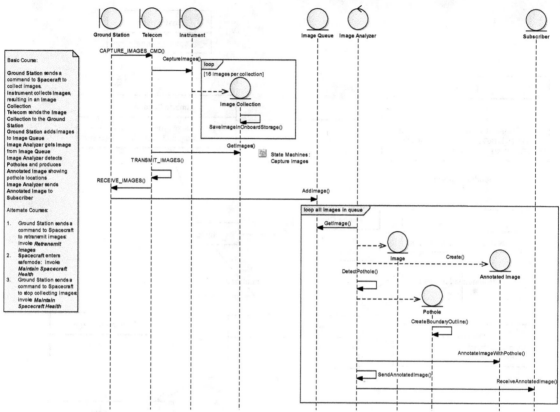

Figure A-11. Sequence diagram shows what the system must do and which elements are responsible for each behavior

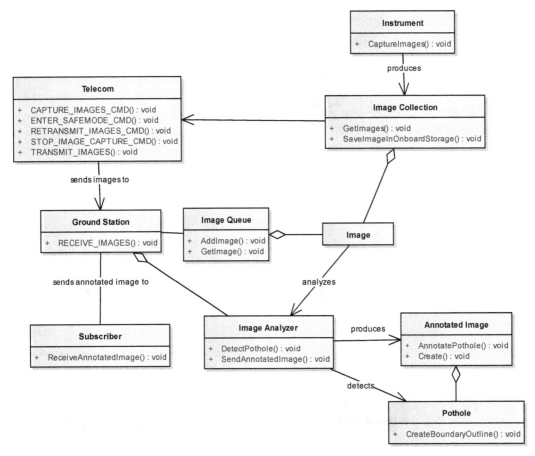

Figure A-12. Expanded Domain Model showing behaviors allocated to system elements

Figure A-13 shows the state diagram for initializing the instrument and capturing images. After initializing buffers and the camera, the instrument enters the Idle state where it waits for a ground command. Receiving a CAPTURE_IMG_CMD causes a transition to the Capturing Images State in which the camera is made ready.

Images are captured and saved by the "do" behaviors. Images are captured in the circular buffer until the STOP_IMAGE_CAPTURE_CMD is received. This command disables the camera after the current image capture is complete and the instrument returns to the Idle state.

Figure A-14 shows a power parametric model comprising camera, data store, telescope, and instrument computer power models. The parametric model sums these components to form a total power usage.

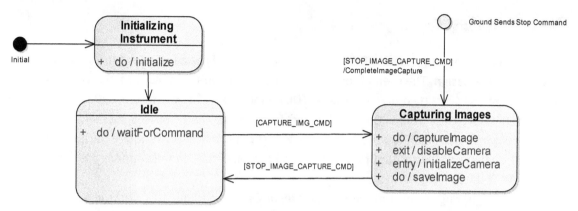

Figure A-13. All states and transitions must be tested

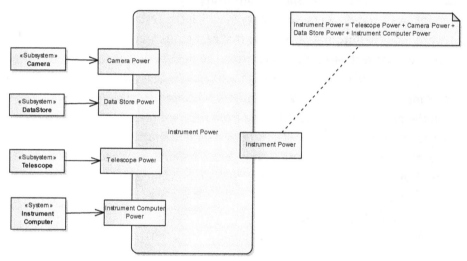

Figure A-14. Instrument Power Parametric Model

This completes our description of basic SysML artifacts and sets up the testing discussion that follows. While our POTHOLE example is simplistic and fanciful, the models we described are the basis for many systems.

The next section describes the baseline DDT methodology and rationale. We follow with a description of an extension for systems.

Design Driven Testing

Stephens and Rosenberg[57] define Design Driven Testing (DDT) as a logical extension to UML-based software design. The premise of DDT is that the bottom-up "agile" practice of driving designs from unit tests (test driven design—TDD) is inherently backwards. In TDD, test cases are developed before code design. Code is then written to make the test cases pass and recoded as necessary if test cases fail. TDD produces a lot of test cases but more seriously because of its ad hoc nature, doesn't fully account for a customer's needs. In fact, the user needs are determined by the test results!

Arguably, ignoring the cost of unnecessary testing and recoding, TDD works in an agile development cycle. However, the type of code produced is not suitable for critical applications and most users can tolerate odd behavior until the next update is pushed out. No one would ever develop spacecraft or any other critical applications using TDD.

The DDT approach follows a top-down methodology in which the testing is automatically generated from software models. Automation assures that test cases aren't missed and the link to software models assures that test cases are driven from the design.

DDT is an appropriate starting place for developing Systems V&V test methods because most system behavior is accomplished in software. We define SysML based extensions to DDT (DDT/Systems) later in the paper. Since we are starting from DDT, we present a high level summary of the approach here, which we will illustrate by example shortly.

DDT automates test case generation for both developers using unit tests and for QA testers using acceptance tests. Figure A-15 shows acceptance test relationships. Mission requirements are driven by customer needs and use case scenarios define what a user does with the system. DDT generates tests that evaluate requirement compliance and correct implementation of desired behavior. As shown in Figure A-16, DDT also applies during the development cycle by automating creation of controller tests from robustness models (see next section) and unit tests.

---

[57] *Design Driven Testing: Test Smarter, Not Harder* by Matt Stephens and Doug Rosenberg (Apress, 2010). Also see: www.designdriventesting.com

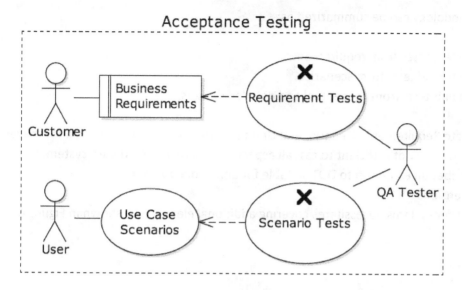

Figure A-15. Acceptance Testing Flow

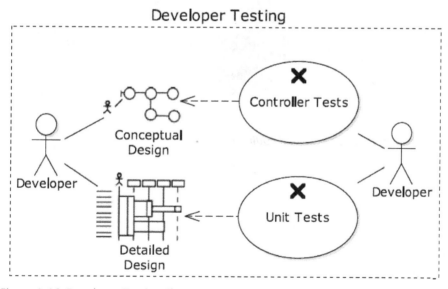

Figure A-16. Developer Testing Flow

APPENDIX A

The DDT methodology can be summarized as:

- Generate test cases from requirements.
- Generate thread tests from scenarios.
- Generate unit tests from conceptual and detailed designs.

We will illustrate Requirement, Scenario, and Unit test generation by example in a few pages. However, these tests are not sufficient to test all aspects of a hardware/software system. Our next section describes an extension to DDT suitable for embedded systems.

DDT/Systems Extensions

Extending DDT for systems necessitates covering additional elements as shown in Figure A-17.

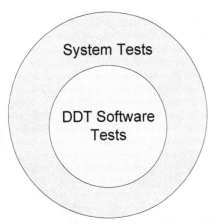

Figure A-17: DDT/Systems includes DDT Software and additional tests

These elements include:

- State Machines
- Activity Diagrams
- Block Definition Diagrams
- Internal Block Diagrams
- Constraint Block Diagrams

Figure A-18 shows the system extensions to DDT.

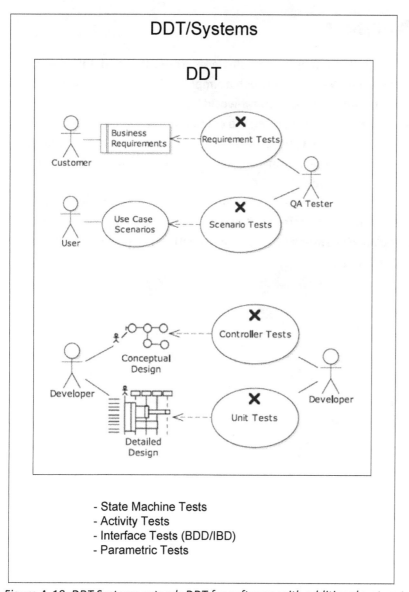

Figure A-18: DDT Systems extends DDT for software with additional system tests

We next apply DDT/Systems to the POTHOLE spacecraft.

Validating POTHOLE with DDT/Systems

We focus our POTHOLE design and V&V examples on a single reference function: taking and processing images for finding potholes. We walk through a simplified V&V process by example in the figures below. The next section summarizes the real-world V&V process.

Now we come to the next validation step: checking the completeness, correctness, and consistency of our use case description. We want to assure ourselves that we haven't forgotten something or specified something too vaguely or incorrectly. Any errors in our use case must be fixed and as necessary and the domain model iterated.

We are now ready to define test cases. We can automatically generate a test case element for every requirement on a requirement diagram, as shown in Figure A-19. Requirement tests are an integral part of the test plan. Generating test cases automatically from all requirements ensures that none are forgotten.

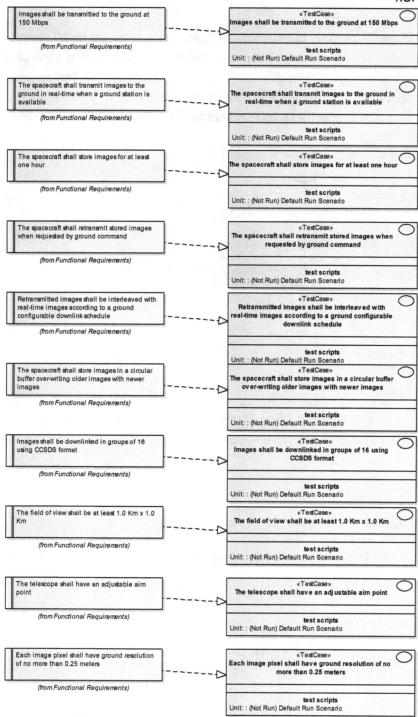

Figure A-19. POTHOLE Mission Requirement Test Cases

APPENDIX A

We use a "use case thread expander" to automatically generate test scripts for all sunny-day/rainy-day permutations within a use case. The premise of this approach is that a use case with one sunny-day scenario and three rainy-day scenarios requires at least four test scripts in order to exercise all usage paths. This process is illustrated in Figures A-20 to A-22. Figure A-20 shows a "structured scenario" that specifies step numbers and "join" logic for our use case.

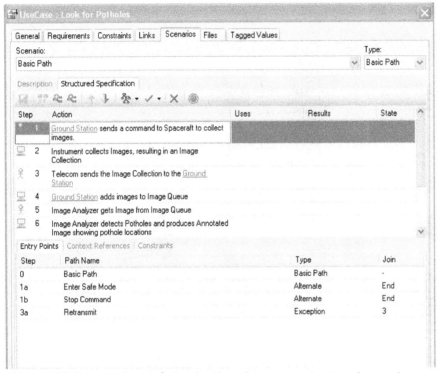

Figure A-20. Expanded sunny/rainy day threads: create a structured scenario

Figure A-21 shows an automatically generated activity diagram that is used to verify the logic of the scenario before tests are generated.

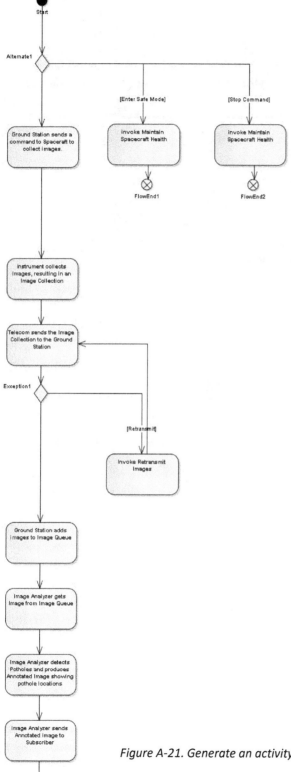

Figure A-21. Generate an activity diagram and check flow against use cases

Figure A-22 shows a test case diagram, showing the complete use case text in a note, and a test case element with a test scenario ("thread test") for each Course of Action within the use case.

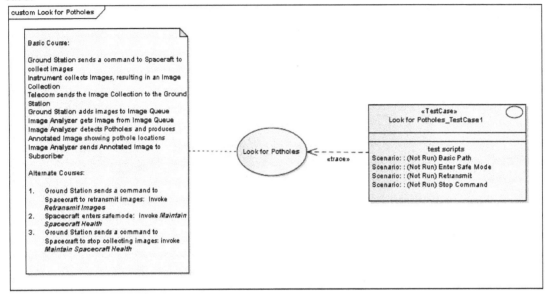

Figure A-22. Scenario Testing

Usage paths are automatically generated for each thread, as shown in Figure A-23. These threads show portions of the Basic Course and portions of the Alternate Courses, as relevant for each thread.

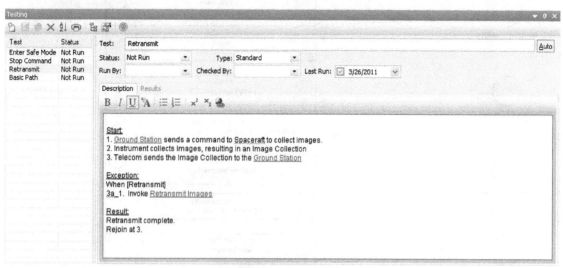

Figure A-23. Generate test scripts from use case text

DDT follows a use case driven approach to design in which each use case performed by the system is first elaborated at a conceptual level (refines the use case and validates the system) and then at a detailed design level (for system verification). DDT generates test case elements from "controllers" on conceptual design (robustness) diagrams, as shown in Figure A-24.

Unit tests are also generated from messages on design-level sequence diagrams as shown in Figure A-25. After test scenarios have been detailed with Inputs, Outputs, and Success Criteria, the test cases are automatically transformed into unit test code suitable for regression testing frameworks such as JUnit, NUnit and FlexUnit. [58]

---

[58] See: www.junit.org, www.nunit.org and www.flexunit.org respectively.

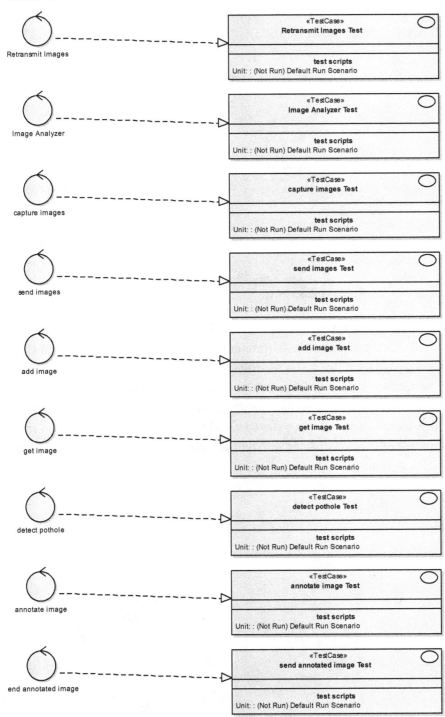

Figure A-24. POTHOLE Controller Test Cases

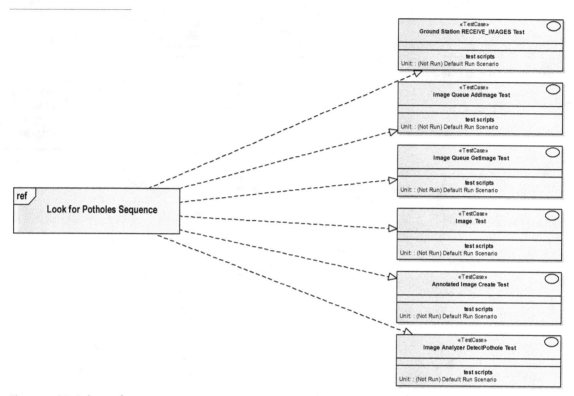

Figure A-25. Subset of Autogenerated Look for Potholes Sequence Message Tests

Figure A-26 shows state, state transitions, and behavior test cases for the capture image state machine described earlier. All behaviors, transitions and triggers must be tested including "entry," "do," and "exit" behaviors on states. Note that similar tests must also be defined for activity diagram behavioral descriptions.

Interface Control Definitions must also be tested. This includes electrical and logical interface definitions as shown in Figure A-27. This includes port, required/provided interfaces, electrical and timing, and fault behavior tests.

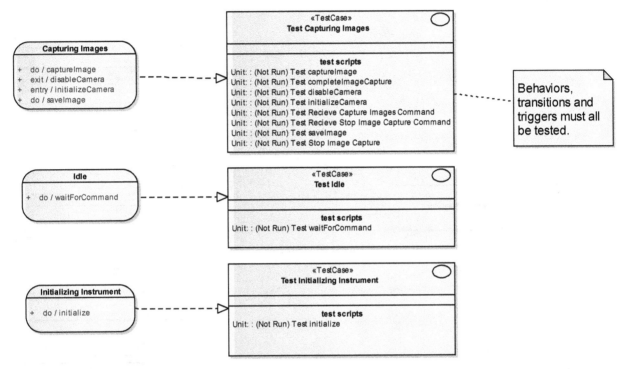

Figure A-26. Examples of state tests

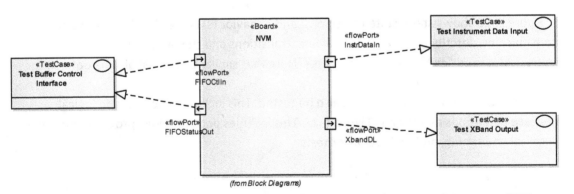

Figure A-27. Need to test all behaviors and interfaces defined in an Interface Control Document (ICD)

In many cases, analytical models are needed for evaluating non-behavioral requirements. These models could evaluate mass, power, radiation effects, and so forth. Figure A-28 shows a parametric diagram that evaluates instrument power. The computed total power is compared to a maximum instrument power requirement.

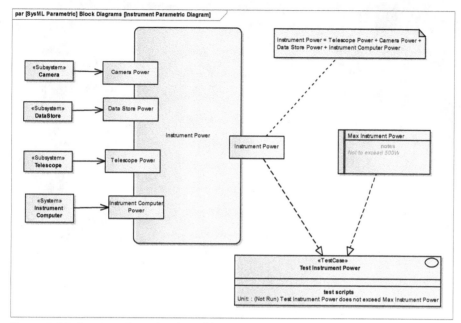

Figure A-28. Parametric evaluation of instrument power

This concludes our illustration of DDT/Systems using the POTHOLE example.

As illustrated in this section, DDT/Systems comprises the following set of tests:

- Requirement tests
- Scenario tests
- Controller tests
- Sequence tests
- State machine & Activity tests
- Interface tests
- Parametric tests

This is the most comprehensive and efficient system V&V approach we are aware of.

Conclusions

- DDT automates generation of test cases from UML models for software
- Systems V&V requires additional modeling and test case generation from SysML
- Our fictitious POTHOLE spacecraft illustrates some of these extensions
- We have described proposed addition to DDT that encompasses systems (DDT/Systems)

APPENDIX B

Business Process Modeling with Structured Scenarios

In 2008, based on our experience with a number of business process engineering projects over the last few years, we developed the *ICONIX Business Modeling Roadmap*; a step-by-step cookbook for Business Analysts (BAs) which details our simplified approach to business modeling. Our roadmap is premised on the idea that BAs want to focus on modeling a business and not on elaborate business modeling notations. We write business process scenarios in an unambiguous vocabulary by defining a model of the problem domain, and we map allocate business requirements to our business processes.

The Roadmap consists of three major activities: *modeling business processes*, *identifying requirements* (and allocating them to the business scenarios), and *modeling the problem domain*. Sometimes we refer to these three activites as "the triangle" (see Figure B-1). We capture information opportunistically among the three activities of the triangle—the exact sequence is unimportant, as long as the information is captured in the model.

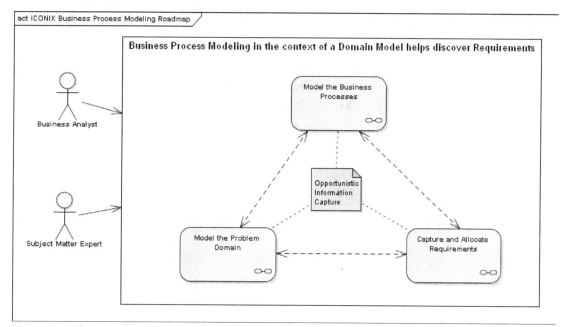

Figure B-1. The triangle of Business Process Modeling

Each of our top level roadmap activities expands out into a child activity diagram. We'll walk through them one at a time in a few paragraphs.

How we Got Here

The Virginia Department of Motor Vehicles has made extensive use of Version 1 of the ICONIX Business Modeling Roadmap. You can view an HTML report of the Virginia DMV Systems Redesign model built using the Enterprise Architect tool, and read a case study of the project on the Sparx Systems website. The DMV model is very large but is still a "work-in-progress." It represents the combined effort of a team of more than thirty dedicated professionals, all working together in one model, with one goal: an effective new system for the DMV to support its full range of internal and customer support activities.

Version 2 of our roadmap, released in 2009, incorporated a significant advance in automation over the first roadmap, namely, the ability to automatically generate an activity diagram from a narrative English description of a business process. This advance in automation was significant because our experience with elaborating scenarios with hand-drawn activity diagrams, while fine "in theory", taught us that this step could be very time consuming, which creates some very real issues "in practice".

This article (which actually represents the third incarnation of our BP Roadmap), leverages two new capabilities from Sparx Systems, available in Enterprise Architect from Version 8 onwards. These are the **Structured Scenario Editor** are the **Business Rule Composer**. The remainder of this article describes how these two quantum leaps in technology combine synergistically to enable a new process. But before we jump into the roadmap, a brief discussion of how business process modeling fits into the overall development lifecycle is in order.

Similarities Between Business Modeling and Software Design

A second premise of our approach is that *business process engineering efforts are usually a precursor to software system design*, and there is a natural desire for a seamless transition between the business modeling process and the software design process which will subsequently be followed.

ICONIX has extensive experience in modeling software projects, and thus we formulated a simple strategy for effective business modeling that transitions seamlessly into software design. In order to explain this strategy, it's important to understand what's similar and what's different between these two endeavors.

Business modeling and software design are *similar* in a number of ways; to begin with both business processes and software designs are best understood by modeling **scenarios** . In both cases, the scenarios that are identified exist to accomplish (realize) **requirements**, which can be either functional or nonfunctional requirements. Some of the functional requirements represent **Business Rules**. The Sparx Business Rule Composer allows behavioral code to be directly generated for Business Rules. We'll discuss this in more detail later.

Also in both software and business models, an unambiguous vocabulary which describes the important "things" (entities) in the **problem domain** is very desirable to avoid ambiguity in the scenario descriptions. The domain model can be used as a precursor to defining a logical data model. There isn't a one to one correspondence between domain objects and database tables, but there will usually be some resemblance.

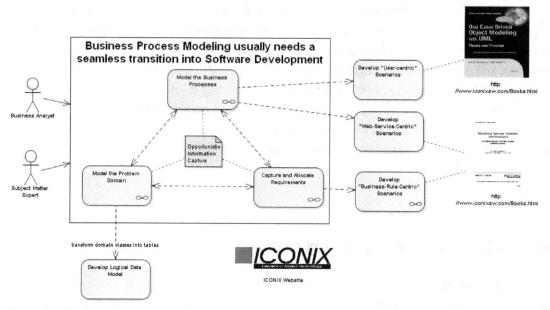

Figure B-2. Business Process modeling exists within the context of software system development

Some business processes might be accomplished manually. Other processes are candidates for automation. Of these, some involve GUI-based software, and others might be realized using web services. ICONIX has other roadmaps for software development, (this roadmap is described in my book Use Case Driven Object Modeling—Theory and Practice), and for Service-Oriented Architecture development (described in the eBook "Modeling Service Oriented Architectures).

Differences Between Business Modeling and Software Design

Business modeling and software designs are *different* in a number of ways; software scenarios (more commonly referred to as use cases) typically involve one or more users interacting with a software system, while business scenarios typically involve a mix of human-computer and human-human interactions, where the human-computer interactions may span multiple software systems.

Business scenarios are often modeled in both "as-is" (existing business) and "to-be" (future business) forms, and it is especially important that business scenarios are well understood by non-technical Subject Matter Experts (SMEs) who understand what the business is about but may not be involved in Information Technology at all.

Software Use Cases should be linked to objects, and also to screens and GUI storyboards— business scenarios do not require this. Elaborating software use cases with conceptual design (robustness) diagrams forces those linkages, and is thus the step we use in ICONIX Process for Software to disambiguate the use cases prior to doing detailed design on sequence diagrams.

In both business and software modeling, first-draft scenarios typically get **elaborated** with a diagrammatic representation of the scenario. There is a learning curve associated with the conceptual and detailed design diagram notations (for example, boundary, control, entity stereotypes) which is easily justified for software designers but is less easily justified for business modeling, which inevitably involves non-technical SMEs. As a result the ICONIX Business Modeling Roadmap specifies that business scenarios should be elaborated with activity diagrams (which are more easily understood by non-technical SMEs) instead of robustness diagrams.

BPM Triangle: Requirements Capture and Allocation

We use Requirement Diagrams to capture and organize **Requirements** . The Roadmap identifies four specific categories of requirements: **Functional** , **Non-Functional**, **Business Rules**, and **Data Requirements** (see Figure B-3). However, these categories are simply meant as guidelines; feel free to group your requirements into whatever categories make sense for your business.

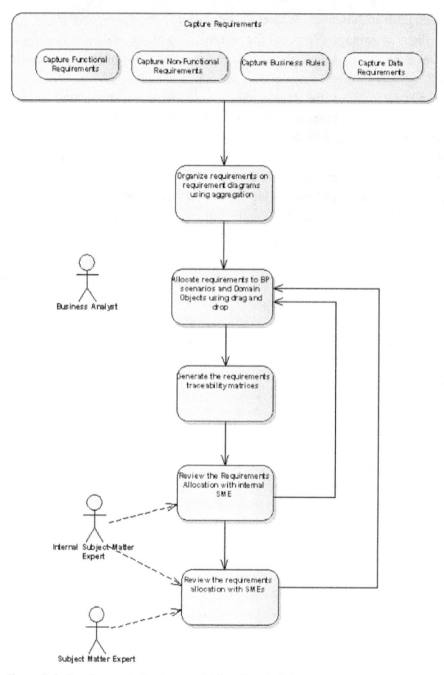

Figure B-3. Requirements Capture and Allocation Activies

Our Roadmap specifies both an *"internal" Subject Matter Expert* (this is someone within the Business Analyst team who is knowledgeable about the relevant part of the business) as well as the *"real" Subject Matter Expert*, who is typically part of the operational business as opposed to a member of the IT staff.

Also note that the Roadmap specifies that Requirements, once identified, should be *allocated* to the business scenarios, and that *traceability matrices* should be generated and reviewed. We have found that the Enterprise Architect (EA) modeling tool does a remarkably good job at automating these activities.

Requirements can be allocated to scenarios using a simple drag-and-drop, and EA's built-in relationship matrix takes all the pain out of generating the traceability reports. Allocating and tracing requirements is critically important to verifying the integrity of the business process models.

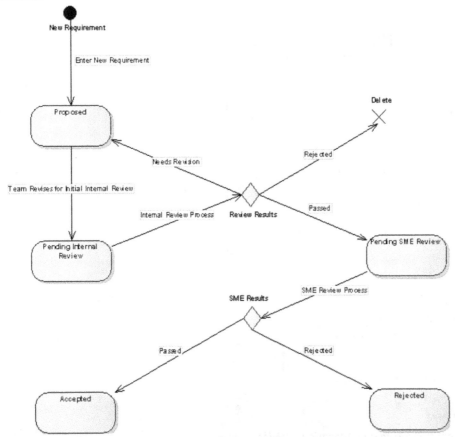

Figure B-4. Requirements are accepted or rejected based on SME Review

BPM Triangle: Modeling the Problem Domain

As with our software design process (standard ICONIX Process), **disambiguation** is of fundamental importance in the ICONIX approach to Business Modeling. Ambiguity in specifications (whether they are at the business scenario or at the software scenario level) often starts with analysts using multiple names for the same "problem domain entity". Therefore the same guidance that we provide in the ICONIX Process Roadmap applies in our business modeling roadmap.

Business Process Scenarios should refer to entities in the problem domain unambiguously, using a well defined and documented name. We show these entities on a domain model diagram (a simplified UML class diagram) which shows the entities along with the "has" and "is" relationships (aka aggregation and generalization) between them.

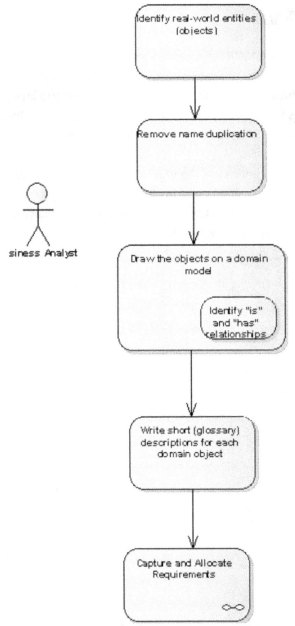

Figure B-5. Modeling the Problem Domain is a critical element of ICONIX Business Process Modeling

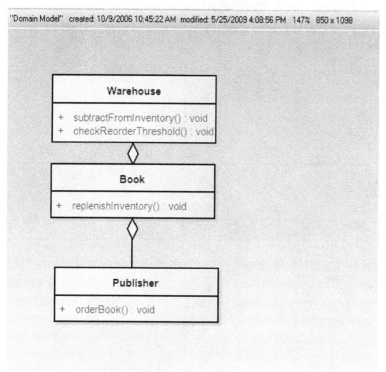

Figure B-6. Example of a domain model.

BPM Triangle: Modeling the Business Scenarios

Modeling Business Process Scenarios represents the bulk of the Business Analyst activity specified by our roadmap. We first decompose the business into **subsystems** (functionally related areas) and show this decomposition on UML package diagrams.

Within each subsystem, we identify the **business scenarios** as stereotyped use cases on UML use case diagrams. As with software scenarios, each business scenario is written in English, and will typically contain both a **sunny-day** (basic course of action) and a **rainy-day** (alternate courses of action) section. It often makes sense to capture both *as-is* (existing state) and *to-be* (future state) business processes. While our roadmap shows the path for future scenarios, the same steps can easily be used for modeling as-is scenarios, which would logically precede the modeling of future scenarios.

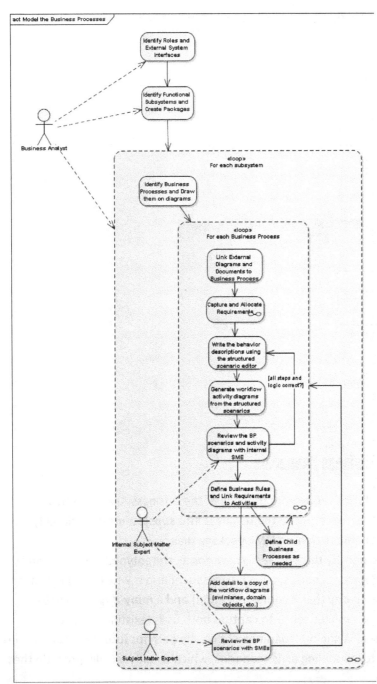

Figure B-7. Business Process Scenarios are identified and documented, requirements are allocated and traced, and the scenarios are elaborated using Activity Diagrams to expose errors.

After the business scenarios have been identified and documented in English, they are linked to requirements that have been identified earlier in the process. Typically additional requirements are identified and captured during this process.

Once the scenarios have been captured, it's generally advisable to <u>elaborate them in diagrammatic form</u>, as (similarly to software scenarios) the act of elaborating a scenario by drawing a picture of it tends to expose errors and inconsistencies.

In Version 1 of the Roadmap, Activity Diagrams were drawn by hand. This led to some practical difficulties in meetings with Subject Matter Experts. This version of the Roadmap incorporates an advance in tools technology—specifically, EA's ability to automatically generate activity diagrams from a Structured Scenario (narrative English) description.

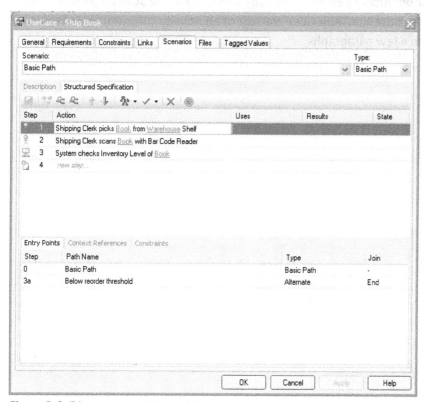

Figure B-8. EA generates UML Activity Diagrams automatically from Structured Scenarios

There are numerous advantages to generating Activity Diagrams from Structured Scenario descriptions as opposed to drawing them manually. These include:

- Time savings
- Ability to review Activity Diagrams with SMEs during JAD session meetings
- Fewer "errors in translation" from scenarios to diagrams
- Improved rigor (identification of branches that have not been considered)

Our experience working with business modeling clients indicates that these are real and important issues, which can have a dramatic effect on the outcome of a BPR project. The Virginia DMV project mentioned at the beginning of this article, for example, has over 3,000 activity diagrams in its UML model.

Figure B-9 shows an automatically generated Activity Diagram for the Structured Scenario shown above. Note that we chose the "RuleFlow" variant of an Activity Diagram, for reasons that will become obvious in a few paragraphs.

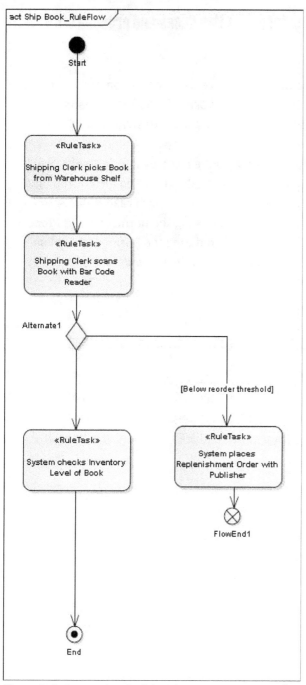

Figure B-9. Generating Activity Diagrams automatically generated from Structured Scenarios saves time and enables better communication with Subject Matter Experts

When User Interaction is Involved, Identify Software Use Cases and proceed with System Design

For those portions of those business scenarios that will involve user interaction and use cases, software will be designed using the use-case driven *ICONIX Process for Software* roadmap. When we have captured and reviewed all of our business scenarios with subject matter experts, we can consider moving forward to implement those scenarios.

In some cases, the future-state business scenarios may be realized by multiple software systems. These automation opportunities should be systematically identified, prioritized, and scheduled. For each new system developed, the software scenarios which realize the business scenarios should be identified and design should proceed following the normal *ICONIX Process for Software* Roadmap. Note that the requirements identified during the business modeling activities should once again be allocated and traced to and from the software use cases.

Model complex business rules and generate "business rule enforcement" code

But some parts of these applications (generally the "back-ends" of the use cases) will be largely created in order to enforce business rules. As a first step in this process, once the Activity Diagrams have been generated, they can be used with EA's Business Rule Composer. This linkage requires the Activity Diagram to be a variant called a RuleFlow diagram, with each activity stereotyped as a RuleTask.

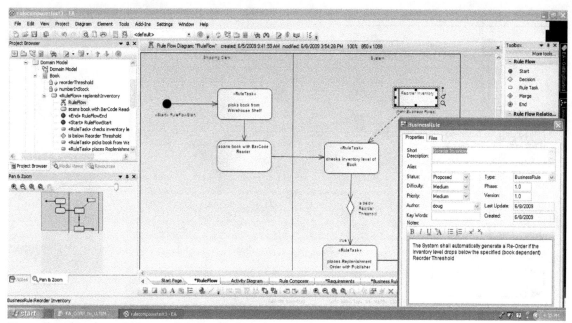

Figure B-10. Business Rules are linked to RuleTasks on the generated RuleFlow diagram

Once the RuleFlow diagrams are generated and the Business Rules linked to the RuleTask Activities, the next step in the process is to define logic for business rules using the Sparx Business Rule Composer.

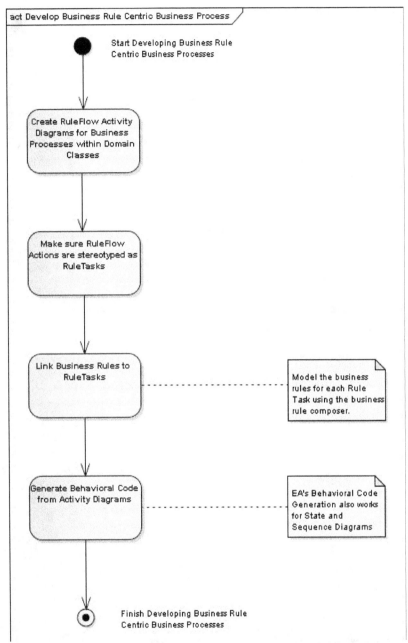

Figure B-11. Our Roadmap combines automatic generation of RuleFlow diagrams with automatic generation of behavioral logic for Business Rules, resulting in a quantum leap in automation for "business rule centric" processes.

The Business Rule Composer allows logic to be specified for a series of "business rule" requirements. This logic can be in the form of decision tables and computational rule tables, and can be quite complex. A key to the process is that the logical steps are tied directly to the business rules.

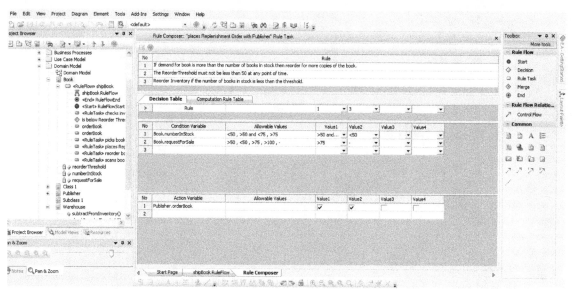

Figure B-12. The Sparx Business Rule Composer defines algorithmic logic for business rules.

The advantages of linking logic to business rules using the rule composer can be readily seen by examining the code that Enterprise Architect generates for these business rules.

Figure B-13. Algorithmic code is generated that is directly traceable to the Business Rules.

Enterprise Architect generates code in a wide range of languages. The example shown here is Java, but could just as easily be C# or Visual Basic. The key to note here is that the generated code contains the logic for each business rule, and the traceability between programming logic and business requirement is directly visible in the generated code. And there are no errors in translation or misinterpretation of the business requirements during implementation.

To summarize, we gain the following advantages:

• Automatic generation of algorithmic logic
• Complete traceability from generated source code to business rule requirements
• Elimination of errors in translation from business model to software model
• Elimination of "cowboy coding" deviation from requirements during implementation

ICONIX has over 20 years' experience working with software projects of all shapes and sizes, and our experience indicates that these issues are definitely of critical importance to development efforts.

Conclusion

The ICONIX Business Modeling Roadmap specifies a simple, intuitive, yet rigorous approach to business modeling and offers a seamless transition to use-case-driven software design when it becomes time to automate portions of the future state scenarios.

Our roadmap also leverages two new advances in tools technology from Sparx Systems that, when used together, enable a new paradigm for the development of "rule enforcement" code that starts with a natural language scenario description and ends up with automatically generated logic that is directly traceable to the requirements.

For further questions, contact us at ***umltraining@iconixsw.com***.

DESIGN DRIVEN TESTING

The groundbreaking book *Design Driven Testing* brings sanity back to the software development process by flipping around the concept of Test Driven Development (TDD)—restoring the concept of using testing to verify a design instead of pretending that unit tests are a replacement for design.

Anyone who feels that TDD is "Too Damn Difficult" will appreciate this book.

Visit the website for more info:

www.designdriventesting.com

Design Driven Testing shows that, by combining a forward-thinking development process with cutting-edge automation, testing can be a finely targeted, business-driven, rewarding effort. In other words, you'll learn how to test smarter, not harder.

OPEN
ENROLLMENT
TRAINING

You've read the book, now get the training!

Learn how to apply the process roadmaps you've just read about in this book from Doug at an ICONIX Open Enrollment workshop

Developers: Learn a rigorous, systematic path from requirements to source code

Business Analysts: Accomplish business process modeling for requirements elicitation and process reengineering

Systems Engineers: Apply a rigorous design and testing methodology using SysML

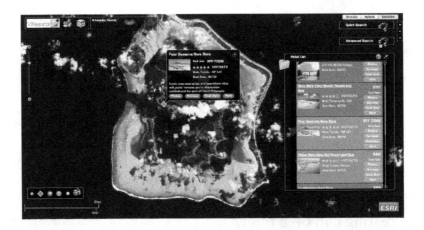

The Design Driven Testing course uses as its example an interactive hotel mapping system which you can try out for real at: www.vresorts.com

For the latest Open Enrollment schedule, please visit:
www.iconixsw.com/EA/PublicClasses.html